THE
SECRETS TO
MAINTAINING
YOUR
DELIVERANCE

ALEXANDER PAGANI

CHARISMA HOUSE

THE SECRETS TO MAINTAINING YOUR DELIVERANCE
by Alexander Pagani
Published by Charisma House, an imprint of Charisma Media
1150 Greenwood Blvd., Lake Mary, Florida 32746

Tyndale House Publishers, Carol Stream, Illinois 60188.
All rights reserved.

For more resources like this, visit MyCharismaShop.com
and the author's website at alexanderpagani.global.

Cataloging-in-Publication Data is on file with the Library
of Congress.
International Standard Book Number: 978-1-63641-402-7
E-book ISBN: 978-1-63641-403-4

01 2024
Printed in the United States of America

Most Charisma Media products are available at special
quantity discounts for bulk purchase for sales promotions,
premiums, fund-raising, and educational needs. For details,
call us at (407) 333-0600 or visit our website at www
.charismamedia.com.

To my daughter-in-law, Yoleiry Pagani; my granddaughters, Laila Rose Pagani and Leilani Grace Pagani; and my future grandchildren to be born to Alex-Xavier Pagani

CONTENTS

INTRODUCTION

DIDN'T I SEE this person in my last mass deliverance event? Isn't this the third time we've taken him through deliverance? How many times is he going to come to the altar to be delivered?"

"I've seen this person on numerous deliverance videos from various ministries. Clearly, she is only looking for attention."

"Why isn't deliverance working for this person? I'm not taking him through another deliverance session."

These were the kinds of thoughts running through my mind after traveling the globe and helping thousands of believers go through deliverance. I would see a repetitive cycle: people being delivered, then asking for re-deliverance, then asking again for more re-deliverance. One day I began to ponder, "Either I'm doing something wrong, or they're not following the protocols to maintain their deliverance."

After much consideration and thought the Holy Spirit revealed to me that I couldn't expect them to maintain their deliverance when I had only cast the demons out but never given people the protocol to keep the door closed in the future. I'd focused on being a surgeon, expertly removing demons, without recognizing that people also needed a clinical doctor—someone to teach them how to prevent demonic activity. Not all doctors are surgeons—but all surgeons are doctors.

Whew, what a powerful revelation! In all these years I had never considered this.

The Bible says that God's people "are destroyed for lack of knowledge" (Hos. 4:6, NKJV). Ignorance is the greatest weapon used to attack many believers who've been set free from the demonic and had generational curses broken. They are still ignorant of the dos and don'ts of post-deliverance maintenance.

When a patient is ready to be discharged after surgery, typically the doctor first meets with the patient, giving him or her a list of rules to follow for a speedy recovery and regulations to observe to prevent the need for further surgery in the future. This book is designed to be just like those rules and regulations. It is meant to give you the secrets to help you stay free after your deliverance (or re-deliverance). So, read on, and you will learn how to hold on to your deliverance and keep the enemy from re-infiltrating your life.

CHAPTER 1

THE TWO MOST SIGNIFICANT SECRETS

He replied, "You are permitted to understand *the secrets of the Kingdom of God.*"

—LUKE 8:10, NLT
EMPHASIS ADDED

But it was to us that God revealed these things by his Spirit. For his Spirit searches out everything and shows us God's *deep secrets.*

—1 CORINTHIANS 2:10, NLT
EMPHASIS ADDED

This message was kept secret for centuries and generations past, but now it has been revealed to God's people. For God wanted them to know that the riches and glory of Christ are for you Gentiles, too. And this is *the secret: Christ lives in you. This gives you assurance of sharing his glory.*

—COLOSSIANS 1:26–27, NLT
EMPHASIS ADDED

I'VE ALWAYS SAID the goal of the deliverance ministry is that you get free and stay free so you never have to come back. Unfortunately such is not usually the case. As the popularity of deliverance ministry has increased in recent years, so has "deliverance idolatry." My prayer has always been to move on from deliverance ministry into other areas of the kingdom where I can serve, but right now it seems that heaven needs me here until the church has normalized deliverance and I can move on. In the meantime I am writing this to help those who read my first two books (*The Secrets to Deliverance* and *The Secrets to Generational Curses*) learn post-deliverance secrets so they can maintain their freedom and steer away from deliverance addiction.

My two previous books are packed with so much revelation that you have to reread them many times to understand, and they have a heavy focus on the demonic to expose the darkness. This book is different. In it I'm going to focus on *turning on the light* by not only emphasizing the freedom that Christ purchased for us on the cross but also placing a high value on Scripture and redirecting you to the person of Jesus. I'm going to give you protocols outlined in Scripture to continue in the truth of God's Word—because the truth will set you free.

The secrets outlined in this book are designed to function much like a user guide for deliverance. Most manufacturing companies include user guides with their products. Each of these handy manuals informs the buyer how to assemble the product, how it works, and how to troubleshoot it if it malfunctions. When it comes to the ministry of deliverance—and any ministry outlined in Scripture—the Bible is our ultimate user guide, and it reveals protocols set in place to ensure ministries function at their optimum through the power of the Holy Spirit. If buyers follow the instructions, they will enjoy the greatest benefit of the product.

Could it be that many believers who experience deliverance never truly maintain it or enjoy their newfound freedom because they haven't spent enough time reading the manual? To be honest, I haven't read the user guides for most of my electronic products, so I've likely never truly enjoyed them to their fullest potential. Heaven wants us to enjoy the freedom found in Christ to its abundance. Jesus declared that He came not to just give us life but to give us life in abundance.

> The thief cometh not, but for to steal, and to kill, and to destroy: I am come that they might have life, and that they might have it more abundantly.
>
> —JOHN 10:10

Another verse I love, which is just as powerful as John 10:10, says this:

> If the Son therefore shall make you free, ye shall be free indeed.
>
> —JOHN 8:36

Or as some have rendered it, "Whom the Son sets free is free indeed"!

Freedom is guaranteed if the believer maintains it (through the person of the Holy Spirit and Scripture) by following the protocols outlined in the user guide to ensure optimal performance. You can be free and stay free. You don't have to live in an endless cycle of receiving deliverance, then undergoing more and more re-deliverance. I'm not opposed to multiple deliverance sessions, but freedom truly must be maintained, and the deliverance sessions should be kept to a minimum.

In this chapter I will begin to explain the secret of the manual and user guide for deliverance. In the coming chapters I will go into further detail about what the rules, regulations, protocols, and instructions are and why God told Moses and Ezekiel to pay close attention to them before allowing the children of Israel—a type, or symbol, of today's Christian—to experience their newfound freedom in the land of milk and honey.

Let's look at the process the children of Israel underwent on their journey from Egypt to the Promised Land and parallel it to the journey of the Christian, especially after one is first born again. God saved the children of Israel from the bondage of slavery in Egypt, and they crossed the Red Sea, just as Christians cross the sea of worldliness by making full repentance of their sins and trusting in the finished work of Christ on the cross. The children of Israel then journeyed through the Wilderness of Sin to Mount Sinai (Exod. 16:1–2). According to Deuteronomy 1:2, the land of Canaan was only an eleven-day journey from Mount Sinai, but God led the people south through the Sinai Peninsula. The text is clear as to why God delayed their entrance to the Promised Land until they were strong and numerous enough: so that the "beasts of the field" wouldn't overtake them and the war wouldn't wear them out (Exod. 23:29–30, NKJV).

The believer is no different. After we become new Christians, God takes each of us through a series of trials and tests to purify our faith and to train us for spiritual warfare, lest the kingdom of darkness (aka the "beasts of the field") overtake us. God took the children of Israel south, to the foot of Mount Sinai, and there He proceeded to give them His manual and user guide. The same is true for Christians; we are also given a manual to guide us in the dos and don'ts of maintaining our freedom in Christ. We have been set free from the grip of the temptations of Egypt and the idolatry in the land of Canaan.

Deliverance is the same. If believers don't know the manual or the principles found in the user guide, they won't know the dos and don'ts necessary to maintain their deliverance and will eventually find themselves needing additional deliverance sessions.

Let's look deeper at the purpose of a user guide and see how it parallels what the Christian uses today (specifically in the ministry of deliverance). Let me give you a definition first.

WHAT IS A USER GUIDE?

A user guide is a set of instructions that "accompanies your product, service or system to the end users and helps them use it." It can be known as a user manual, a product manual, or an instruction manual. "The goal of a user guide is process documentation"—meant to help end users better understand the product through step-by-step instructions. These instructions provide "detailed information about a product's operations, functionalities, standards and guidelines, troubleshooting and more."[1] Because of that, it's usually the first document the buyer consults before using the product.

It is my firm belief that the reason the ministry of deliverance is misused or abused is that most believers who experience deliverance are not told what to do afterward, nor is there typically a follow-up plan to accompany them after their freedom is secured. The Bible makes it clear that after receiving freedom, a believer *can* be put in bondage again:

> So Christ has truly set us free. Now make sure that you stay free, and don't *get tied up again in slavery to the law.*
>
> —GALATIANS 5:1, NLT
> EMPHASIS ADDED

Other translations of this verse use the phrase "entangled again." This doesn't mean these believers will lose their salvation. Entanglement is not a salvation issue but a practical sanctification issue. Let me repeat this: *Entanglement is not a salvation issue.* I want each of you to know that your salvation is intact, by the power of the Holy Spirit. The struggles you're dealing with do not alter the status of your salvation. You might experience discouragement in your daily walk with Christ, but you are seated with Christ in heavenly places (Eph. 2:6). I assure you that by the time you reach the end of this book, you will be equipped to maintain your deliverance—and you will have matured so that you need deliverance only when the Holy Spirit is truly guiding you to make an appointment for a session.

Let's dig deeper into our user guide. Obviously, the user guide is the Bible, but the instructions aren't easily discovered. Why? Because the Bible says this:

> It is the glory of God to conceal a matter, but
> the glory of kings is to search out a matter.
> —PROVERBS 25:2, NKJV

Heaven wants to know whether you're serious about your *resolve* or just seeking *relief*. *Relief* means you're looking only for a temporary, quick Band-Aid solution because you're currently being tormented; you want a way out of your current situation, but you don't intend on repenting, surrendering to Christ, and living a life submitted to the Word of God. If you are ready to *resolve* the situation, you are among those who are tired of the endless cycle of getting free but not staying free—who are truly ready to resolve the demonic issues in their lives, close the door on those issues, and live according to Scripture, maintaining their liberty.

The user guide that teaches you how to maintain

your deliverance is hidden in a secret—as is every answer you're looking for from God. Why? So those who are truly hungry will rise to the occasion, search the secret out, and then find it. The Bible says:

> Ask, and it shall be given you; seek, and ye shall find; knock, and it shall be opened unto you: For every one that asketh receiveth; and he that seeketh findeth; and to him that knocketh it shall be opened. Or what man is there of you, whom if his son ask bread, will he give him a stone? Or if he ask a fish, will he give him a serpent? If ye then, being evil, know how to give good gifts unto your children, how much more shall your Father which is in heaven give good things to them that ask him?
>
> —MATTHEW 7:7–11

This text lets us know that heaven is willing to grant us the revelation to the hidden things—but we need to persevere. In this book I'm going to share the secrets I discovered for my own life that caused me to walk in utmost victory in Christ. They also helped me move away from being so deliverance-conscious to being Christ-centered and

Scripture-based. You must pursue. Heaven is trying to reveal to you what is hidden in secret. Will you put in the effort to discover these truths?

PAYING THE PRICE

Hidden in the package of almost every product is a user manual, but until you *pay the price* of sacrifice (buy the product), you will never access what's inside the box. A price must be paid before the secret is revealed. The question I ask you is this: *How hungry are you to maintain your freedom?* What are you willing to give up to ensure that your freedom in Christ is enforced? Jesus paid the ultimate price, sacrificing His very life, to make you free, *but you must also count the cost necessary to enforce that freedom.*

Many people in the deliverance community frequently misquote the following verse:

> And ye shall know the truth, and the truth
> shall make you free.
>
> —JOHN 8:32

What many overlook is the clause in the verse that precedes these words. But this clause is important because it contains the little word *if*.

Jesus says:

> If ye continue in my word, then are ye my
> disciples indeed.
>
> —JOHN 8:31
> EMPHASIS ADDED

Your true freedom is predicated on continuing in God's Word, meaning there are rules, regulations, protocols, and instructions regarding truth that you must carry out before your freedom is ensured. If you're ready to learn these instructions, then pray the following prayer:

> *Heavenly Father, thank You for setting me free from the devil's grip through the atoning sacrifice that Jesus accomplished on the cross. Thank You that You have equipped me through Scripture to use the weapons of my warfare. Holy Spirit, I humbly ask You to give me insight and revelation as I read this book so I can effectively use those weapons and stand fast in liberty, for Christ has made me free. In Jesus' name, amen.*

THE SECRET REVEALED

Let's further explore the idea of a secret. I know, especially in recent years, the word *secret* often has negative connotations. Yet numerous verses throughout Scripture use this word, and in most, if not all, it has a positive meaning.

The issue with the word *secret* lies not in the concept of secrecy but in the idea of trust. Secrets are shared with those who display the utmost trust, confidence, and worthiness. When someone chooses to share a secret, it's not because the sharer is showing partiality but because the recipients have earned the right to be entrusted with the information—the sharer knows they are mature enough to receive it and will value it.

One of the Hebrew words translated as "secret" in the Old Testament is *sod*, which indicates "talk about something to be kept confidential"—that is, a "confidential conversation" (such as in Amos 3:7).[2]

Merriam-Webster defines the word *secret* as "something kept from the knowledge of others or shared only confidentially with a few; a method, formula, or process used in an art or operation and divulged only to those of one's own company or craft: trade secret."[3]

If you value your freedom in Christ, then heaven is ready to give you confidential information that the Lord reveals only to those who are trustworthy enough to receive it. We will talk about untrustworthiness in later chapters, because we must address deliverance addiction. But for now let's explore these secrets heaven wants to give you.

Some people ask, "Does God want to give us these secrets?" The answer is a resounding *yes*. In Matthew 13 we see Jesus telling the apostles that it was *God's will* to give them the secrets of the kingdom because they had the paid the price; they had made the sacrifice in leaving everything to follow Him. These secrets are what made the apostles victorious over evil, the devil, and the world during their time with Jesus and on their apostolic journeys.

> He replied, "You are permitted to understand *the secrets* of the Kingdom of Heaven, but others are not."
>
> —MATTHEW 13:11, NLT
> EMPHASIS ADDED

This verse has been my heart's cry and prayer in everything I do in ministry. I want to know the secrets of the kingdom. The apostles gave up everything to follow Christ, and as a result, permission was granted for them to learn the secrets of heaven. Here is the directive: Live a life that is so pleasing to God that permission will be granted to you to experience the abundant life in Christ.

You might be thinking these "secrets of the kingdom" were given only to the Twelve and those who walked with Him and that we were not to desire or seek after them. Well, the apostle Paul in many of his New Testament epistles says quite the opposite. He tells us in 1 Corinthians 2 that it is the will of God to reveal these secrets to us by the Holy Spirit, who has been given to us as our earnest, or deposit:

> That is what the Scriptures mean when they say, "No eye has seen, no ear has heard, and no mind has imagined what God has prepared for those who love him." But it was to us that God revealed these things by his Spirit. For his Spirit searches out everything and shows us God's *deep secrets*.
>
> —1 CORINTHIANS 2:9–10, NLT
> EMPHASIS ADDED

This verse makes it very clear that New Testament believers who genuinely love the Lord will be shown God's deepest secrets, by will of the Holy Spirit (the Revealer of secrets). It's clear that heaven is not trying to hide these secrets; instead, the Father desires to reveal them to those who are genuinely seeking and won't cast heaven's pearls before the swine.

I want to share one more passage regarding secrets, which I think is the clearest biblical reference that reveals the true heart and vision of this book. It is meant to help believers who have experienced the beautiful ministry of deliverance to not just get free but also maintain their freedom:

> The secret of the LORD is with them that
> fear him; and he will shew them his cove-
> nant. Mine eyes are ever toward the LORD;
> for he shall pluck my feet out of the net.
> —PSALM 25:14–15

These verses make me want to shout, because they have a twofold meaning: If you are a believer who fears the Lord (which I'm assuming you are if you are reading this book), then there are secrets heaven will reveal to you as you read. The second verse then says that these revealed secrets will help you pluck your feet out of a trap. Hallelujah! There is no reason any recipient of deliverance ministry shouldn't consistently receive heaven's intelligence about how the world, the flesh, and the devil are working against him or her—and then escape their traps.

THE TWO KEY SECRETS

In my first book, *The Secrets to Deliverance*, I gave readers insight into the operation of demons in the human realm to help them find resolution for the toughest cases of demonic bondage. In my second book I went deeper into exploring the generational curses that keep our bloodlines bound. At this point any person who has read both of those books should be walking in some sort of freedom. I spent much time exposing the hidden treasures of darkness because it was heaven's desire to reveal those things. Take a look at the following verse:

> And I will give thee the treasures of darkness, and hidden riches of secret places, that thou mayest know that I, the LORD, which call thee by thy name, am the God of Israel.
> —ISAIAH 45:3

As you can see, heaven doesn't want God's people to be ignorant, and revelation concerning the kingdom of darkness is available if we search for it. As we noted earlier, the Bible says it is the glory of God to conceal a matter, but it's the honor of kings to search the matter out (Prov. 25:2).

So, again, in my first two books I spent an enormous amount of time describing in detail the realm of the demonic—how demons and generational curses interact, and so on. But in this book I'm going to shift and move in a different direction. Instead of exposing the darkness, I'm going to turn on the lights. When the lights are turned on, the darkness is dispelled by default. This leads me to share with you the first secret.

SECRET 1: YOU HAVE GOD'S ARMOR OF LIGHT

Most believers are aware of the armor of God—you can read about it in Ephesians 6. Yet the Bible goes a step further in describing the nature of these protective coverings by collectively calling them the *armor of light*. Take a look at the following verse:

> The night is far spent, the day is at hand: let
> us therefore cast off the works of darkness,
> and let us put on the armour of light.
> —ROMANS 13:12

I love this verse because it encourages us to stop overemphasizing the works of the devil. Instead it admonishes us that "the night is far spent" and that we are to cast off the works of darkness by changing our thinking—from darkness-centered to light-focused. Along with this armor of light that we are to put on comes the guarantee that we can remain in a perpetual state of freedom, without becoming what I call a "deliverance junkie."

What are deliverance junkies? They are people who refuse to take responsibility to crucify their flesh; who fail to close all doors in their lives that are open to the flesh, the world, and the devil; and who blame the devil for any consequences of their own laziness. Instead of repenting for any sin and doing the necessary work to keep their lives clean, they are quick to run to deliverance sessions. They shy away from actual repentance, accountability, and responsibility, and rather than putting on the armor of light, they continue to blame-shift everything on demons. Oh, that believers would shift their deliverance worldview away from extreme demon-consciousness and toward the gospel and what's been given to us through Jesus' work on the cross! We would see a decreasing emphasis on the ministry of deliverance and an increasing emphasis on the ministry of preaching the gospel of the Lord—which is our primary commission.

I mentioned in my first book that deliverance is not a power encounter but a truth encounter. The devil and his demons prefer to dwell in the dark. There is no light in the devil—only darkness. In fact in John 8:44 the Bible tells us that he is not only a liar but also the father of lies. This lets us know that our primary battle with the kingdom of darkness is that of *truth* versus *lies*. The truth can be found only in the Light (Jesus), so by contrast, lies are found in the darkness.

Wearing the armor of light will provide us with tremendous protection against the enemy of truth. Light dispels the darkness; at the presence of light, the darkness flees. Therefore, wearing the armor of light will bring more preventative freedom than confrontation. We are to submit to God first and *then* resist the devil (while wearing the armor of light), and he will flee (Jas. 4:7). If more Christians would wear this armor, they would begin to experience more and more victory in their daily lives.

So, how do we put on the armor of light? Here are three ways to do this, along with scriptures to support them.

The Light of the Word

The Bible says, "Thy word is a lamp unto my feet, and a light unto my path" (Ps. 119:105). When believers hold a high regard for Scripture, over and above demons, curses, and any other work of darkness, the light of God's Word shines on their paths, and they don't stumble. When we turn to Scripture first in all we do, then the light of truth begins to push out all the forces of darkness, and all the enemy's lies (including fiery darts) begin to fall by the wayside. We need to start verbally affirming Scripture over our lives each morning when we first wake up and each time we leave our homes, drive our cars, work at our jobs, deal with our children, face challenges, get bad medical reports, feel the devil attacking our minds, and so on. In essence we must take up the armor of light, and when we do so, the lies of the enemy lose their power.

> For he raised us from the dead along with Christ and seated us with him in the heavenly realms because we are united with Christ Jesus.
>
> —EPHESIANS 2:6, NLT

An example of this can be found in the Book of Ephesians. We are seated with Christ in heavenly places, far above all principalities and powers (Eph. 1:20–21). We can affirm this positional truth as we carry out our day-to-day activities by making the following declaration. Say this out loud:

> *Father, I thank You that in Christ, I am seated with Him in heavenly places, so I have no need to be fearful of the kingdom of darkness today—because the devil is under my feet.*

Wow! I felt the power of God hit me as I wrote that—because it's true. Use the space provided to write out how this declaration made you feel.

_____

_____

_____

_____

The Light of the Spirit

One of the symbols of the Holy Spirit is light. The person of the Holy Spirit is given to the believer as the Paraclete, meaning "one called to the side of another."[4] The Holy Spirit illuminates our path and leads us, guiding us into all truth (John 16:13). When a believer is being led by the Spirit, they are being led by light. In the following verse Jesus actually calls the Holy Spirit within us "living light":

> Jesus said to the people, "I am the Light of the world. So if you follow me, you won't be stumbling through the darkness, for living light will flood your path."
>
> —JOHN 8:12, TLB

Being led by the Spirit of light is a huge defense against the wiles of the wicked one (Eph. 6). The Holy Spirit doesn't just live inside your heart; when you are surrendered to Him, He will be an armor of defense to cover your whole being. In a sense you will become untouchable. I find it hard to believe that demons would constantly attack you if you were full of the Holy Spirit and truly walking in the light. This is why the Bible talks about the importance of walking in the light:

> But if we walk in the light, as he is in the light, we have fellowship one with another, and the blood of Jesus Christ his Son cleanseth us from all sin.
>
> —1 JOHN 1:7

Right now, as you read this, surrender to the person of the Holy Spirit, and ask Him to surround you with light as part of your armor of light. Trust me, He will do it, and no devil in hell will be able to penetrate the defense He raises up around you.

The Light of Purity

I have learned the principle of purity through my years of walking with the Lord, especially during a season of consecration I found myself in not too long before I wrote my first book. I was allowing the Lord to make my heart pure, in accordance with the Beatitudes, where Jesus said, "Blessed are the pure in heart: for they shall see God" (Matt. 5:8).

One day when I read this verse, I received a huge revelation that pureness of heart causes clarity in the Spirit. If there is anything the deliverance crowd struggles with, it is seeing God clearly to properly diagnose what kind of battle they are facing. If I wrote a book on misdiagnosis within the ministry of deliverance, I think it would end up being several volumes long—there is that much material to cover. Yet being pure of heart lights up our perceptions, motives, and intentions, making it crystal clear for us to see into the spirit realm. Jesus said that the pure of heart would see God. As we secure our freedom in Christ, so much confusion comes from a lack of being pure in every area of life. When I allowed God to purify my perception, my discernment increased, and I could distinguish between right and wrong very quickly.

To put it another way, we must allow God to purify our understanding. Let's look at one more scripture that will drive this point home:

> Your eye is like a lamp that provides light for your body. When your eye is healthy, your whole body is filled with light. But when it is unhealthy, your body is filled with darkness. Make sure that the light you think you have is not actually darkness. If you are filled with light, with no dark corners, then your whole life will be radiant, as though a floodlight were filling you with light.
>
> —LUKE 11:34–36, NLT

The Greek word for "eye" in verse 34 can be used "metaphorically, of the eyes of the mind."[5] And Ephesians 1:18 refers to "the eyes of your understanding being enlightened"—indicating that our understanding has eyes, or perception. (What a powerful revelation!) It is critical, then, that we make sure the eyes of our understanding are healthy so we can have 20/20 vision. Anything other than 20/20 vision would be considered unhealthy eyesight.

In the Luke 11 passage Jesus tells us that if our eyesight (our understanding) is healthy, then our whole bodies will be filled with light. It's unfortunate that so many deliverance folks (as I like to call them) do not have a healthy understanding of deliverance; they "fire walk" in darkness more than in the light. Their blindness affects their practical sanctification, and they are distracted by the demonic, which allows extremes and fanaticism to often creep in. (We will deal with that in later chapters.)

Verse 36 is key, for it tells us what will happen if we are "filled with light"—the light of sanctification, which shines into the realm of the mind and soul. We don't want bodies with "dark corners," which are areas in our souls that haven't yet been fully purified by heaven. These areas could include our motives, intentions, values, and so on; they don't affect our salvation, but they do affect how we maintain our freedom.

These are the three ways you can begin to put on the armor of light: focus on the light of the Word, the light of the Spirit, and the light of purity, and shine each of those brighter in your life. This is by no means an exhaustive list of ways we can do so, but it's a good start.

It seems that most believers who are in the deliverance crowd don't put all three of these strategies into practice; probably only a select few are that comprehensive. Why? Maintaining their deliverance requires them to take some personal responsibility in freeing themselves rather than become deliverance junkies. For the rest of us who are serious about getting free and staying free, these three steps must become part of our daily lives.

With the help of the Holy Spirit, let's put on the armor of light, live in the light, be led by the light, be cleansed through the light, and live the victorious, abundant life.

SECRET 2: CHRIST IS IN YOU

I wish I had emphasized the second secret more throughout my years of ministry, but I myself got caught up in the trend of deliverance (and if I'm honest, I, too, overblamed the devil). This is why I'm writing this book now, to *under*blame the devil and reclaim our personal accountability in the maintenance of our deliverance. In doing so, let's begin to place a high emphasis on Scripture again and incorporate it in our daily lives.

So, what is this secret? Let's take a look at the following scripture:

God has given me the responsibility of serving his church by proclaiming his entire message to you. This message was kept secret for centuries and generations past, but now it has been revealed to God's people. For God wanted them to know that the riches and glory of Christ are for you Gentiles, too. And *this is the secret*: Christ lives in you. This gives you assurance of sharing his glory.

—COLOSSIANS 1:25–27, NLT
EMPHASIS ADDED

The King James Version of verse 27 uses the phrase "Christ in you, the hope of glory." What I'm about to disclose to you will be one of the most important revelations you will receive, superseding anything else I write in this book. It's this: *Christ is in you.* Let me say that again: The secret is *Christ in you.*

This one revelation will cause you to stand firm in your freedom more than anything else. Christ is living inside us. And when Christ is living inside us, we can then walk that out. Every demon, devil, and generational curse must return to hell where it came from.

The secret hidden all throughout history was

that at an appointed time the eternal Son of God would live inside His people, causing them to walk victoriously over the flesh and the devil. When believers truly embrace the truth that Christ is living on the inside, they begin to realize that the same Spirit who raised Jesus from the dead lives in their mortal bodies (Rom. 8:11). This same Jesus—who conquered sin, death, and the grave—dwells within each of us. Wow! *That changes everything.* The demon phobia that grips many believers who seek deliverance dissipates, and a new holy boldness strengthens them. They begin to walk boldly, knowing that "greater is he that is in [them], than he that is in the world" (1 John 4:4).

This same revelation of Christ in you is what the early church experienced in the Book of Acts. They had no preoccupation with signs and wonders. But when they truly understood that Christ lived within them, the victorious and miraculous became their normal way of life.

And guess what? *Christ in you* cancels out the need for multiple deliverance sessions. I'm not saying you shouldn't seek deliverance if you need it; I have experienced six sessions during my own

Christian journey. But once I began to understand the riches of Jesus' glorious inheritance in the saints, deliverance sessions for me became far less frequent.

Repeat after me out loud: "Christ in me, the hope of glory." Now, didn't that feel good to affirm? Speak this out loud one more time so the demons of hell can hear you. Then say it as many times as you need to, until it sinks into your mind.

THE GOSPEL OF JESUS IS ENOUGH

The gospel of Jesus means "good news." What's the good news? That Jesus paid the penalty for all your sins, was buried, and three days later was resurrected from the dead. His resurrection not only declares complete freedom for the believer but also brings perpetual freedom. *Satan lost his power at the cross* (Col. 2:14–15; Heb. 2:14). The gospel is enough. *Jesus* is enough.

The gospel removes the endless cycle of deliverance sessions and codependency on deliverance ministers. The gospel removes that feeling of tirelessly needing to seek more deliverance. *The gospel makes you perpetually free.* Any ministry that makes it appear that being a Christian should bring about an endless phobia of demons and a constant need for deliverance is teaching and preaching heresy. Deliverance is a by-product of the gospel, and it is required only when individuals have discerned that they've lost control and need help through deliverance sessions.

> For he has rescued us from the kingdom
> of darkness and transferred us into the
> Kingdom of his dear Son.
> —COLOSSIANS 1:13, NLT

At this point you might be tempted to say that with the revelation of these two secrets, there is no need to read the rest of this book. *Don't fall into the trap* (like many do) *of reading only the first part of the user guide and not its entirety.* Christ in you is the foundational secret from which all other secrets in this book will draw their revelation. There is much left to learn, and I have much to reveal to you from all my years in the deliverance ministry—especially some of the mishaps that caused me to lose my deliverance and to need to seek it again. Let me pour into you with this, my third book. You'll be surprised at what you will learn and which direction I will take.

But now we have begun with the two main secrets—the armor of light and Christ living in you—which is the best and most important place to start.

Pray this prayer together with me, and let's trust that the Holy Spirit will continue to speak to you throughout the rest of this book:

> *Heavenly Father, I thank You for revealing Your two most important secrets to the church. As I am part of the church, I thank You that Christ lives in me and that You have equipped me with Your amazing armor of light. Lord Jesus, I humbly ask You to strengthen me with might by Your Spirit in my inner being so I can victoriously walk in all the secrets of the kingdom. Thank You, Holy Spirit, that You will lead me, guide me, and cover me with the light of Your presence. In Jesus' name, amen.*

CHAPTER 2

THE SECRETS OF DIVINE ENABLEMENT

Son of man, describe to the people of Israel the Temple I have shown you, so they will be ashamed of all their sins. Let them study its plan, and they will be ashamed of what they have done. Describe to them all the specifications of the Temple—including its entrances and exits—and everything else about it. Tell them about its decrees and laws. Write down all these specifications and decrees as they watch so they will be sure to remember and follow them. And this is the basic law of the Temple: *absolute holiness! The entire top of the mountain where the Temple is built is holy. Yes, this is the basic law of the Temple.*

—EZEKIEL 43:10–12, NLT
EMPHASIS ADDED

By his divine power, God has given us everything we need for living a godly life. We have received all of this by coming to know him, the one who called us to himself by means of his marvelous glory and excellence. And because of his glory and excellence, he has given us great and precious promises. These are the promises that *enable you to share his divine nature and escape the world's corruption caused by human desires.*

—2 PETER 1:3–4, NLT
EMPHASIS ADDED

The Father...has *enabled you to share in the inheritance that belongs to his people, who live in the light.* For he has rescued us from the kingdom of darkness and transferred us into the Kingdom of his dear Son.

—COLOSSIANS 1:12–13, NLT
EMPHASIS ADDED

IN MY FIRST book, *The Secrets to Deliverance,* I described the parallel of the temple of Solomon to the human "temple," aka the human body. Ezekiel 43:10–12 is a clear symbol of the need to help God's people understand how the human body works in regard to spirituality and freedom. Some key points and concepts may seem like a repetition of the content of my first book, but they are essential in understanding what God is saying.

What is God's purpose for the believer, according

to Ezekiel 43? *Absolute holiness.* Some synonyms for the word *absolute* are *definite, utter, decisive, complete, outright.*[1] This means that heaven isn't playing around with your personal sanctification. Heaven has decreed that holiness must be incorporated in your life. This level of submission to the Word and to Christ will increase your resistance level to demons, and you will no longer need multiple deliverance encounters (except in extremely severe cases). Yet this level of consecration must be purposeful and intentional. You can't wait for it to appear; you must actively pursue it. If there is one attribute I wish more of the deliverance crowd had, it is a determination to pursue—that is the missing ingredient necessary for them to stay demon-free. In the Book of Galatians, the Bible instructs us to "stand fast therefore in the liberty wherewith Christ hath made us free" (5:1). The act of standing requires work; it requires effort. It requires endurance to stand and not be moved. (I will get into this in more detail in the next chapter.)

The word *absolute* also implies having no partiality in holiness. In other words, we are not 60 percent holy to 40 percent unholy, or even 70 to 30 percent. No, heaven is requiring *complete* holiness with *all* areas of our lives surrendered to the dictates of Scripture and the presence of Christ. When believers do this, no door will be open for any demons to enter or for any curses to affect their lives. The need for deliverance from demons and curses is so prevalent today because so many Christians live lukewarm, mediocre lifestyles of compromise. Christ Himself rebuked this way of life in Revelation 3 when addressing the Laodicean church.

Unfortunately many in the deliverance crowd want everything to be handed to them. They want the deliverance workers to cast the devil out, help them break every generational curse, and do all the submitting to God and resisting of the devil for them. The moment they are confronted and held accountable to the reality that *they* need to put in some of the work, they leave offended and go find another deliverance ministry. (I will be dealing with all of this in upcoming chapters.)

In His foreknowledge God knew that because of the fall, human beings would need to be taught the ways of holiness. This is why He gave Ezekiel very detailed instructions concerning how he was to help the children of Israel achieve the level of absolute holiness God desired for them as a nation. Keep in mind that this was written while the nation of Israel was in a seventy-year exile period in Babylon. By the time God began to speak to Ezekiel, the Israelites had been compromising and mixing with the hated Babylonian system. They were losing their distinction of being a holy nation, separate unto God. During their time in Babylon a new generation was emerging, and the Law of Moses that had once guided the civil, ceremonial, relational, and spiritual aspects of their lives was being watered down. At one point God rebuked the priests for their inability to even distinguish between clean and unclean:

> Your priests have violated my instructions and defiled my holy things. They make no distinction between what is holy and what is not. And they do not teach my people the difference between what is ceremonially clean and unclean. They disregard my Sabbath days so that I am dishonored among them.
>
> —Ezekiel 22:26, nlt

The verse is clear: they lost their ability to discern holy from unholy. And when discernment is lost, it opens wide the door to the world, the flesh, and the devil. One of the fastest ways you can lose your deliverance is through a lack of discernment. Countless times, believers have come to multiple deliverance sessions for freedom after ignorantly reopening the door to the demonic. The Book of Luke is clear about this problem. Let's read:

> When an unclean spirit goes out of a man, it goes through dry places seeking rest. Finding none, it says, "I will return to my house, from which I came." When it comes, it finds it swept and furnished. Then it goes and brings seven other spirits more wicked than itself, and they enter and dwell there. And the last state of that man is worse than the first.
> —LUKE 11:24–26, MEV

Believers who have just experienced deliverance do not have to fall into the trap outlined in this passage. The best way to ensure that doesn't happen is to follow the instructions given to Ezekiel. In Luke 11 we can clearly see that the demon referred to the man as "my house." But what did God say about the temple of Solomon? He called it "My house" (Ezek. 23:39; 44:7, NKJV). (I dedicated an entire chapter to discuss this in more depth in my first book, *The Secrets to Deliverance*.) It's safe to say the owner of the house—the man—through ignorance either failed to lock the door or left the door wide open, allowing the same spirit that had been cast out to come back. I'm going to give the man the benefit of the doubt; as a homeowner myself there are times when I accidentally forget to lock the door, or I forget there are a million other ways a thief can enter my home. Simply locking the doors and windows isn't always enough, and this is the reason many of us have alarm systems in our homes. Truly the best way to protect your home (your temple) is to know everything about it so you can properly secure all entrances and exits from thieves breaking in.

How can a believer lose deliverance? By not following the instructions in this passage:

> Son of man, *describe* to the people of Israel the Temple I have shown you, so they will be ashamed of all their sins. Let them *study* its *plan*, and they will be ashamed of what

they have done. Describe to them all the *specifications* of the Temple—including its entrances and exits—and everything else about it. Tell them about its *decrees* and *laws. Write down* all these specifications and decrees as they watch so they will be sure to remember and follow them. And this is the basic law of the Temple: *absolute holiness!* The entire top of the mountain where the Temple is built is holy. Yes, this is the basic law of the Temple.

—EZEKIEL 43:10–12, NLT
EMPHASIS ADDED

Describe

The first thing that needs to be done is to *describe*. The meaning of the Hebrew word is "to inform of" or "explain."[2] I find this word so crucial because a lot of what goes on in the deliverance ministry isn't thoroughly explained from beginning to end. A huge emphasis is placed on casting out demons, even identifying any generational curses, but not enough time is spent explaining what got the individuals to the point of needing deliverance or how to maintain their freedom after deliverance sessions.

God wanted Ezekiel to empower the children of Israel by way of explanation. When things are explained and understood, the hearers can take better precautions against the enemy because they understand how things work. The opposite can also be true: when things are not explained, they aren't valued, and irresponsibility tends to result. God told Ezekiel to explain to the Israelites the spiritual temple, with its entrance and exits, as this would cause them to see where they'd been irresponsible and to repent for not properly taking care of the temple. My prayer is that as you read this book, you also will take more seriously the need to protect the entrances and exits of your temple (including your eyes, ears, nose, mouth, and so on). All these areas can be entryways for demons if they are not properly and zealously guarded through Scripture, prayer, and trust in the presence of Christ.

Along with the temple's entrances and exits, verse 11 mentions "everything else about it," which indicates there are other, less common areas of entry. I love this because it gives us room to explore and share new insights that the Holy Spirit gives us in these areas. Trusting in the Holy Spirit is the only way to successfully protect and maintain your deliverance. Earlier the Spirit of God had drawn Ezekiel's attention to a small hole in the temple's wall and told him to dig. When Ezekiel did, he discovered a door leading to a hidden room where all kinds of idolatry were happening in secret. In the same way, our own ignorance gives the devil access to areas in our lives that cause us to lose our freedom in Christ.

> Then he brought me to the door of the Temple courtyard, where I could see a hole in the wall. He said to me, "Now, son of man, dig into the wall." So I dug into the wall and found a hidden doorway....So I went in and saw...the various idols worshiped by the people of Israel.
>
> —EZEKIEL 8:7–8, 10, NLT

Description or explanation also provides opportunity for more emphasis on the *details*. In some instances overlooked details can give a demon entry or allow it to remain hidden. Now you can see why God wanted Ezekiel to describe the temple in detail. An old idiom says, "The devil is in the details." This is so true; even though most believers assume the devil moves *only* in their gross sins, sometimes it is the "little foxes" that ruin the vineyard (Song of Sol. 2:15).

Keep in mind that I'm not describing a paranoia where we fear that anything we do will give the devil an opening to enter—that's bondage. The Bible says that "greater is he that is in [me], than he that is in the world" (1 John 4:4). Nor am I talking about becoming demon obsessed, looking for and finding a demon under every rock. No. I'm just pointing out that we should be more mindful of our surroundings because the devil prowls about "like a roaring lion, seeking whom he may devour" (1 Pet. 5:8, NKJV).

Let's ask the Holy Spirit now to begin to *describe* the areas of entry that aren't frequently discussed. We do not want to be ignorant of ways the enemy of our souls could gain advantage. I will try my best to describe them in this book, but this won't be enough, as I can share with you only the few secrets I have learned throughout the years. However, if you press in to the Holy Spirit, He will continue to share with you the things you need to know—picking up right where this book leaves off.

Pray this with me:

> *Holy Spirit, You are the Spirit of truth. I ask You to reveal to me any areas in my life where I might have overlooked or ignored anything I should be watching out for. Just as You told Ezekiel to pay attention to the small hole in the wall, please help me pay attention to any descriptions You share as I work to guard my life from the traps of the enemy. In Jesus' name, amen.*

Write It Down

One of the best ways to remember things is to write them down. As humans we tend to forget very quickly, or we allow the cares of this life to cause important things to slip our minds. The power of writing helps us not only remember what's important but also document what needs to be passed on to others. God wanted Ezekiel to write down the descriptions of the temple so both the present generation and future generations would not forget and repeat the sinful acts of their ancestors. Writing ensures that the message continues to live on beyond the messenger. Here we are, about 2,600 years later, still reading what Ezekiel wrote in his book.

This will be my third book on the topic of deliverance, and my personal prayer is that all of them will become classics, go-to resources on deliverance. The secrets I will highlight in the upcoming chapters of this book are not the norm for those who have read other deliverance resources, but they are meant to be a user manual with instructions to explain each part of maintaining our freedom.

Specifications

What are specifications? The word *specification* means "a detailed precise presentation of something or of a plan or proposal for something."[3] In essence it involves a true, focused definition of an item or event.

Here is where the problem lies. Many worldviews—including our views on deliverance— are steeped in superstition and not true biblical knowledge. Deliverance ministries can sometimes have more warped concepts than any other group within Christendom. (I'm speaking as the leader of one of those ministries.) Many of our beliefs about how doors in our lives open to demons are misguided because we do not know the specifics. The Holy Spirit wants to show us these specifics regarding areas where demons can enter our lives. Emphasis on a specific instruction gives us a better understanding of that area, and we can guard it better.

Ezekiel 43:11 refers to specifications about the "entrances and exits" (NLT), which means we need to explain what those entrances and exits are, getting into the particulars of how they function. This requires time, because there are a lot of potential entryways. For example, many churches focus only on having Christians guard their hearts, minds, and souls, and they ignore teaching about the other areas where an unclean spirit can enter or reenter. So, believers' hearts may be strong, their minds in order, and their souls stable, but meanwhile the devil is wreaking havoc on their bodies. This is why Paul told us to present our *bodies* as living sacrifices. Our bodies are just as important as our hearts and minds:

> Dear brothers and sisters, I plead with you to give your bodies to God because of all he has

done for you. Let them be a living and holy sacrifice—the kind he will find acceptable. This is truly the way to worship him.
—ROMANS 12:1, NLT

There is a *specific* way to treat your body. Paul knew this, saying he disciplined his body to bring it under control:

I *discipline* my body like an athlete, training it to do what it should. Otherwise, I fear that after preaching to others I myself might be disqualified.
—1 CORINTHIANS 9:27, NLT
EMPHASIS ADDED

When you begin to learn the specifics about areas that are vulnerable to the enemy, you will start to master them. In the Spirit we must learn how to maintain those areas, controlling them through the presence of God and the power of Scripture. *Only through the person of the Holy Spirit can these specific areas be disciplined.*

Now, identifying these specifics is one thing, but understanding what governs them and how they function is another. Ezekiel was also commanded to learn the decrees and laws so he could then teach them to the children of Israel.

Decrees (Ordinances)

At this point my spirit is getting excited because I've been an advocate of the idea that deliverance is not a religious experience but a *legal exchange*. And once believers begin to view freedom from a legal perspective, *everything changes*. I am so glad for this shift away from a moral and relationship lens to a legislative one.

The word *decree* in Ezekiel 43:11–12 is the Hebrew word for "ordinance."[4] In certain contexts the synonyms *rules* and *regulations* can be used in place of *ordinances*.[5] Each entrance or exit has certain rules and regulations that govern it, and if a person violates those rules, he or she shouldn't get angry at the consequences. Just as city ordinances apply only in certain locations, these ordinances aren't written in stone and do not apply to everyone; rather, they are personal rules designed for a specific person or situation.

Let's use eyes as an example. The Bible says that our eyes can be filled with lust; it even uses the phrase "the lust of the eyes" (1 John 2:16). If the

Scripture is clear that our eyes have a propensity for lust, it's our responsibility to make sure we set up some rules and regulations to protect our eyes from lusting. Such rules could include watching no R-rated movies, avoiding late-night hours spent alone on the phone, and staying away from situations that would cause lust after someone other than a spouse. These rules are something believers must set up for themselves, not expect God to do it. Heaven won't stop the world from revolving because a believer has an issue with lust. No. The Holy Spirit empowers you to establish standards and remove yourself from the enemy's snares that, if fallen for, provide an opening for demonic powers to enter.

God's rules are meant to be protective, not restrictive. They are designed to protect believers, not hinder them in what they do. I'm referring not to legalism but to a system of rules designed to surround us with enough barriers and blockages so it is difficult for us to reopen doors or give any place to the devil (Eph. 4:27).

Laws

Ezekiel 43:11 distinguishes a law from a decree or ordinance. The term *law* "refers to a system of rules that regulate the conduct of a community, and is often enforced by a controlling authority through penalties."[6] Such systems of rules also regulate procedures.

How can this apply to entrances and exits? Let's again use the example of the eyes. What is the law—the system of rules regulating the conduct—of our eyes? Our eyes are designed to see; that is the "law" of the eyes. Thus when I hear believers praying, "Lord, control my eyes," I realize they are asking to violate the law of seeing that God established. This is why many times after praying such prayers, they still watch pornography, which opens the door to lust. They then begin to question God, not understanding that this happened because God already set up a law that governs the eye.

In addition the ears are governed by a law of hearing, so if you want the doors to your soul to be closed to the enemy, *you* must stop listening to music or other media that doesn't glorify Christ. There will never be a moment when an ear prompts the believer to stop listening to certain kinds of music, gossip, etc. The ear was created to hear; God set up this law of hearing to govern it.

Another example of a law is the law of touch. God created the human body to react to touch, and when this is governed by the Holy Spirit, it can be a beautiful thing. I love holding both my granddaughters in my arms. The law of touch activates my love for them. I love hugging my younger son when I return from long periods of preaching away from home. It activates the spirit of fatherhood in me. When I see my wife cooking in the kitchen, I love to grab her and embrace her. Why? The law of touch activates my love for her.

Yet this law can also have a negative side. It's best that two Christian singles who are currently in courtship not touch each other frequently, as this will activate feelings that could lead to sin. Many singles have tried to be overly spiritual, asking *God* to "stop them from going further." Well, sometimes that works, but on most occasions the law of touch is governing both of their bodies, and the Bible tells us to "flee fornication" (1 Cor. 6:18)—not to pray about it.

The same principle goes for all our entryways and exits. The Holy Spirit doesn't govern those specific areas, but God's laws do. And if there is one thing I have learned, it is that God's laws will work if you work them. In other words you must take control of the areas that God gave you to control, and then you can let Him do the rest.

Study Its Plan

Now we know why God gave Ezekiel these laws, regulations, and stipulations to govern the spiritual temple in his vision. A user manual won't magically deposit all its information into your understanding; *you must study it*. Without studying the manual, you won't gain all the benefits of the product, and you run the risk of causing malfunction or damaging the product as well. In the same way, you must study how to maintain your deliverance.

I know that this might not be the type of information you were expecting to learn from a deliverance book, but it is so important. In the same way Scripture tells us to study to show ourselves approved to God when it comes to doctrine (2 Tim. 2:15), we must also study how the human body operates regarding spiritual warfare.

If not, we can be doomed to an endless cycle of never-ending deliverance sessions. God wants more for you. He wants you to be studious so you're not caught off-guard in ignorance of the devil's devices.

> Lest Satan should take advantage of us; for we are not ignorant of his devices.
> —2 CORINTHIANS 2:11, NKJV

I'm not telling you to do anything that we seasoned deliverance ministers aren't doing or haven't mastered ourselves. We all had to learn to become avid students of the deliverance ministry, including how to maintain our freedom, and let me tell you—it works. So, how can you transition into this militant deliverance lifestyle (including everything mentioned previously), especially when it might not be part of your nature, character, or personality? The answer is found in the next secret: we are partakers of His divine nature.

SECRET 3: YOU ARE A PARTAKER OF THE DIVINE NATURE

The following passage is one of my favorites. Why? Because it reminds us to stop *overblaming* the devil and start taking *personal responsibility* for our actions. Now, you may have expected me to over-saturate you with brand-new revelation of demons and their names or some new demonic force being released on the earth. While there is a place for that, it is more important that we learn how to close any openings the enemy might want to take advantage of. We do this by obeying what God tells us in His Word. Let's take a look:

> By his divine power, God has given us every-thing we need for living a godly life. We have received all of this by coming to know him, the one who called us to himself by means of his marvelous glory and excellence. And because of his glory and excellence, he has given us great and precious promises. These are the promises that enable you to share his divine nature and escape the world's corrup-tion caused by human desires.
>
> —2 Peter 1:3–4, nlt

Right here it tells us, clear as day, that heaven has given us everything we need. This removes the need for some special revelation or impartation. The atoning sacrifice of Jesus on the cross is more than enough.

Heaven gave us everything we need to live a victorious life over the world, the flesh, and the devil—and especially demons. Demons don't want us to live godly lives. They specialize in tarnishing our lives *when we open doors to let them in.* And then they work hard to make sure we lose our deliverance. It is possible to maintain our freedom when we become aware that by placing our faith in Christ, we experience an exchange. Breaking free from the devil's grasp is impossible without it. The promise given to us in the exchange is this: we are now partakers of Christ's divine nature. This means that our spirits are born again and regenerated through the power of the Holy Spirit, which causes us to be distinct from the world system. The Bible says that "as he is, so are we in this world" (1 John 4:17); our precious Lord lived above the cares of this world, and in the wilderness of temptation He was able to overcome the devil. *That means we can overcome too.* We don't have to be slaves of this world's system.

Our spirits have been re-created by the Spirit of God, and God dwells inside us. The "furniture" in our "house" has been changed. The lustful desires we used to have are no longer there. Therefore, the kingdom of darkness has no right in our lives—unless we give the enemy and his minions permission to enter. If those who have gone through deliverance truly want to *stay free*, they can—because God's very Spirit lives inside them.

You might have noticed the passage from 2 Peter says that because we become partners with Christ, we will escape the devil's corruption. Hallelujah! That is wonderful news. Yet the Bible also says the whole world lies under the enemy's influence:

> We know that we are of God, and the whole
> world lies under the sway of the wicked one.
> —1 JOHN 5:19, NKJV

Despite this obvious fact, you don't have to live in bondage. You may be in this world, but you are not *of* this world (John 15:19). Jesus said:

> They are not of the world, even as I am not
> of the world.
> —JOHN 17:16

I'm not trying to oversimplify things with some quick-fix solutions. And I know you're not accustomed to being told that you're a partaker of God's divine nature—but this one truth and the promises it brings make understanding this and walking it out so worth it. It will enable you to escape the world's corruption. Not only will it cause your walk to be victorious, but it will also destroy your human desire to sin. This means that demons won't be able to tempt you using your human desires to open the door. *Praise God!* You will be able to confidently say, like Jesus' powerful statement here, that the devil has *nothing* in you:

> The prince of this world cometh, and hath nothing in me.
>
> —JOHN 14:30

Make this declaration out loud:

> *Heavenly Father, I thank You that at the cross, You re-created my spirit and made me born again. I am a partner of Your divine nature. This is why the devil has nothing in me anymore. Thank You that Your divine nature causes me to walk out my deliverance. I am victorious over the devil and every demon. Thank You that I am not addicted to deliverance, nor am I a deliverance junkie. Thank You that every*

*door to the enemy was closed in my deliver-
ance, and they will stay closed through the
power of the Holy Spirit.*

SECRET 4: HE HAS ENABLED YOU

Why is partaking of Christ's divine nature so
important? Because it is part of our inheritance. I
mentioned this in the previous chapter concerning
the armor of light. Look how the following passage
continues this same line of thinking:

> The Father...has *enabled you to share* in the
> inheritance that belongs to his people, who
> live in the light. For he has rescued us from
> the kingdom of darkness and transferred us
> into the Kingdom of his dear Son.
> —COLOSSIANS 1:12–13, NLT
> EMPHASIS ADDED

The text says that God has enabled us "to share."
Let's consider a bit of a wordplay here. Yes, this
could refer to something being shared *with you*,
but the verse is discussing something *legal* here, as
in shares, or portions. This is why the word *inheritance* is used, as no inheritance can be distrib-
uted unless the heirs have been allotted shares in

it (the legal right to receive it). *To enable* means "to give legal power, capacity, or sanction to."[7] When you are enabled, we have the legal right to receive what's rightfully yours. In other words the legal right enables you to partake in your inheritance.

What is your inheritance? The text indicates you have an *inheritance of light*; this is why verse 13 says that through salvation, we've been transitioned out of the kingdom of darkness into the kingdom of God's dear Son. This transfer removes false ownership and restores legal rights to human beings—all of whom were lost at the fall of humankind in the Garden of Eden. This has not been restored for an egocentric purpose, in which believers live lavish Christian lifestyles filled with material blessings they demand from God. No, the salvation of our souls gives us the right to live demonically free—both to be freed through deliverance and to remain free thereafter. You've been enabled because you no longer belong to Satan; you belong to Christ!

If you have just gone through your first deliverance session, know that could potentially be your last if you understand and follow everything

I'm teaching you through the scriptures shared in this book. Isn't that great news?

GREATER IS HE WHO LIVES IN YOU

When a believer has truly responded to the gospel and rests in the finished work of Christ, completed on the cross, the same Spirit that raised Jesus from the dead lives inside that person. Jesus defeated Satan and his demons at the cross. His Spirit now dwells in the heart of each believer, causing us to be secure, knowing that He who lives in us is far greater than the enemy of our souls that is in the world. The Holy Spirit revealed this truth to John so all believers can be secure in their minds and spirits concerning their freedom. You've already won, so stand on your victory!

> But you belong to God, my dear children. You have already won a victory over those people, because the Spirit who lives in you is greater than the spirit who lives in the world.
> —1 JOHN 4:4, NLT

How is that for the first part of the user guide for deliverance? We've completed the first two chapters; throughout the rest I will share various secrets for those who have just been delivered, so they know what they should be walking in to remain free, as well as other biblical truths that heaven wants me to include regarding the ministry of deliverance. These secrets are not in any sequential order; rather, as the Lord placed these truths on my heart, I wrote them here.

Let's continue by asking the Holy Spirit to take us deeper and show us more.

> *Holy Spirit, You are our Guide into all truth. Thank You for bringing me through the first two chapters in this book. I humbly ask You to help me continue with the rest of the book and enable me to understand more secrets of the kingdom. I want to know how to walk in the glorious inheritance of the saints. In Jesus' name, amen.*

CHAPTER 3

THE SECRETS OF PREVENTATIVE MAINTENANCE

Stand fast therefore in the liberty wherewith Christ hath made us free, and be not entangled again with the yoke of bondage.

—GALATIANS 5:1

EMPHASIS ADDED

Submit yourselves therefore to God. Resist the devil, and he will flee from you.

—JAMES 4:7

EMPHASIS ADDED

Since you have been raised to new life with Christ, *set your sights* on the realities of heaven, where Christ sits in the place of honor at God's right hand. *Think about* the things of heaven, not the things of earth. For you died to this life, and your real life is hidden with Christ in God.

—COLOSSIANS 3:1–3, NLT

EMPHASIS ADDED

REMEMBER THAT I am not the one who created the secrets I'm presenting here—God did. However, what should never be a secret is repentance. *Everything starts with repentance.* Repentance is actually at the core of the gospel. You must repent of your sins and believe in the finished work of Christ on the cross to be saved. If you don't start at the cross, you're headed down the dark path described in Matthew 7:22, in which those who claimed to be faithful (but weren't) called out, "Lord, Lord, have we not...cast out demons in Your name?" (NKJV).

Jesus died for your sins, and His resurrection breaks the power of sin, the world, and the kingdom of darkness. This regeneration causes you to truly be born again, and it then helps you live a life of holiness, with all doors closed to the enemy. Colossians 2:14–15 says Jesus disarmed the ruling principalities and powers through His death on the cross. In response to this grand act of grace and mercy, repentance is necessary. Repentance means a person does a 180-degree turn (not a 360-degree one); it means changing one's mind and turning to go the other way.

Why am I telling you this at the beginning of this chapter? If you truly repent, you will not return so quickly to those things that will open the door to the devil. Repentance takes place not just at the moment of salvation; it is also a daily experience we commit to through prayer. Many people who come for deliverance haven't yet crossed that threshold of repentance.

In recent years I have switched my *modus operandi* (the way I operate) when it comes to deliverance, in that I no longer immediately delve into it every time I'm asked for help. Now I do more digging and inquiry before I initiate a deliverance session. I start with a set list of questions to determine whether I should engage in warfare for the person. This protects all involved from wasting time, as well as from potentially stirring up a hornets' nest of demons manifesting within the person's life, if he or she is not ready to follow through after a session. This is what I call my Relief vs. Resolve Test. (I have talked about this previously in my other two books, but I think it needs to be referenced again.) The answer I receive lets me know whether the person is really looking for the *resolution* of a situation or simply wants temporary *relief*. (Temporary relief removes the demons only for a short season; without the person's accountability they will reenter his or her life, according to Luke 11:24–26.)

If you're going to stay free, you must resolve never to open the doors to the demonic again. You must be determined to get free—and stay that way. Any deliverance you undergo is a waste of time if you won't get aggressive to maintain your freedom. We are told to stand fast, and the word *fast* means to attach securely, or fasten—like when a nail is driven into wood, it is now fastened to that wood and firm. The NIV and other translations tell us to "stand firm" (from the Greek *stēkō*, meaning "to persevere, to persist"[1]) because Christ has set us free.

In his well-known spiritual warfare discussion in Ephesians 6, Paul used another Greek term for *stand firm (istēmi)* that carries a military sense:[2]

> Therefore, put on every piece of God's armor so you will be able to resist the enemy in the time of evil. Then after the battle you will still be *standing* firm. *Stand* your ground,

putting on the belt of truth and the body
armor of God's righteousness.

—EPHESIANS 6:13–14, NLT
EMPHASIS ADDED

So, we are to stand firm, to persevere, like soldiers committed to a battle strategy created by their military leader. We can't do that if we refuse to take the responsibility to remain solid and steadfast in the areas I'm going to describe in this chapter.

To enforce this level of standing on God's Word requires submission—to God's battle strategy; to your Chief Commander, Jesus; to fellow soldiers who may be in charge of you; and so on. This is why submission is so crucial in standing firm and maintaining your freedom. The biblical concept of submission to God is key before any spiritual maintenance can be done. Why? The Scriptures give us a promise that submitting to God will help us resist the enemy (also implying that we must resist anything in opposition to Him):

Submit yourselves therefore to God. Resist
the devil, and he will flee from you.

—JAMES 4:7

In my opinion this verse could be the most important biblical reference concerning protection against the wiles of the wicked one. (See also Ephesians 6:11.) If Christians would just obey the instructions in James 4:7, there would be far less need for deliverance ministry. This scripture verse is not at war with the understanding that Christians may have a demon, but putting its preventive strategy into practice will help believers stay protected against the kingdom of darkness as well as maintain their freedom after deliverance.

Note: *when you are both submitting to God and resisting the devil, more often than not, you will not need a deliverance session—and you will be able to maintain your deliverance long term.* This is the most important point I make in this book. In fact I'll put it this way so it's easier to remember: *when submission to God is executed, the need for a deliverance session is executed.* (Did you catch the wordplay there?)

Let's go on a brief tangent regarding the rampant failure of many believers in submitting to God, as demonstrated by their lack of obedience to Scripture. We see this in declining church attendance and a general unwillingness to submit to local church leadership. I've encountered a large percentage of "deliverance addicts" who aren't attending a local church, nor are they truly being held accountable by a local presbytery or church leader. This poses a huge threat to the maintenance of their freedom from demonic oppression, because believers can't administer spiritual authority if they are not under authority themselves. The story of Jesus and the Roman centurion made this very clear, as the centurion said, "I am a man under authority" (Matt. 8:9). When believers are not under the protection of the *ekklesia* (the local church), they become "open game" for the attacks of the enemy or leave themselves prone to deliverance errors. In his farewell address to the Ephesian elders (church leaders) in Acts 20, the apostle Paul admonished them to protect and guard the sheep (v. 28)—implying that there is a level of spiritual protection when a believer is a member of a local church and submitted under a local shepherd.

Submission to God and the church looks different for each person, for the Holy Spirit knows what each one of us needs in our lives to guard and protect us in our personal sanctification. *However,* all believers, from every theological persuasion, must follow certain foundational rules or truths, which we will discuss below, to help guard and protect themselves. (You'd be surprised at how many in the deliverance crowd don't practice the secrets I describe. These secrets are truly some of the fundamental responsibilities Christians are to practice, but somehow they have gotten lost in translation with the compromised, lukewarm Christianity we have in today's society.)

Before we get into the deeper secrets in the coming chapters, I think it is necessary to outline more of the foundational disciplines that I believe are essential to maintain your freedom. You might already follow some of these, but you may need to be stirred up to remember the others. The apostle Peter told the church that he wanted to stir them up by reminding them of things they already knew (2 Pet. 1:12–13, NKJV). How many times have you been blasted with an impartation of strength to overcome a sin in your life or press in deeper to the things of God when someone reminds you of scriptures you've read or heard preached or teachings you've listened to about a million times that give you insight about what you need to do? It's like strength then comes out of nowhere to help you overcome in that area.

As I reference and highlight some of the following secrets, you will receive an impartation of strength to obey the Scriptures. I have applied these secrets to my life, and truthfully, I now hardly ever need a deliverance session. I've experienced a total of six deliverance sessions during my walk with Christ— some while serving in the pastorate, especially when I used to preach against deliverance. But that's another story.

I believe this chapter will be extremely beneficial for you, so don't get tempted to breeze through it. Instead internalize the referenced scriptures, and view them as a continuation of what we learned in James 4:7. They are part of God's instructions for preventive protection again the wiles of the devil.

In 1 Thessalonians the apostle Paul prayed that the believers in Thessalonica would be sanctified, meaning separated and fit for the Master's use, in three major areas—body, soul, and spirit—and that, as a result, they would be "preserved blameless" before the Lord. This text goes above and beyond in telling us again that *all areas* of our lives can be *completely preserved* from demonic attack:

> And the very God of peace sanctify you wholly; and I pray God your whole spirit and soul and body be preserved blameless unto the coming of our Lord Jesus Christ.
> —1 THESSALONIANS 5:23

In the rest of this chapter we will look at guarding these three areas—spirit, soul, and body—and some others I feel are necessary as a foundation to maintain your deliverance. Let's start with the spirit first.

SECRET 5: MAINTAIN YOUR SPIRIT

Guarding your spirit is the most important thing you can do as a Christian. The Bible has many things to say about the human spirit. First, if it is wounded, it dries up one's bones (Prov. 17:22). In other words when your spirit is affected in a negative way, the issue goes deep inside and causes instability in your life. It feels like the world is weighing you down, just like when those who have physically weak bones can't carry a heavy load because the pressure is too much. When our spirits are wounded, we lose the will to fight. Not only that, but the Scripture says a person who can't control his or her spirit is like a city without walls (Prov. 25:28)—meaning one's defenses are low and any intruder can come in. This is why *you must maintain the strength of your spirit*. Let's learn more about this.

The Filthiness of the Spirit

Because 1 Thessalonians 5:23 tells us it is God's intention to preserve our spirits as blameless, we can rest on His promise to do so. However, we must also colabor with Him in that process, making it our business to *not allow our spirits to become filthy*. I use the word *filthy* because it implies an external issue, in contrast with *corruption* or *contamination*, which denotes an internal problem. Because the believer's spirit is one with the Holy Spirit, and the present work of the Spirit of truth continually sanctifies us, our spirits remain intact due to our oneness in Christ.

Note: This is why true Christians can never be demon-possessed. Their spirits have been born again and regenerated through the power of the

Holy Spirit, due to their repentance and faith in Christ. Believers are one with Christ, and no demon can ever cross that border. Hallelujah!

Yet the following verse implies that although a believer's spirit is untouchable at its core, it can still be made filthy:

> Because we have these promises, dear friends, let us cleanse ourselves from everything that can defile our body or spirit. And let us work toward complete holiness because we fear God.
> —2 CORINTHIANS 7:1, NLT

This seems to reflect what Jesus said to Peter in John 13 while washing His disciples' feet. At first Peter protested, but when Jesus reminded him that cleansing was necessary in order to follow Him, Peter urged Jesus to wash his whole body, not just his feet. That's when Jesus said to him, "Those who are clean don't need to take baths; they just need to wash their feet. I have already cleansed you through the Word, so only your feet need to be washed." (See John 13:10.)

I truly believe Paul had this statement from Jesus in mind when he wrote to the Corinthian church. In 2 Corinthians 4:16, Paul said that our "inward man [the human spirit] is being renewed day by day" (NKJV). This renewal is accomplished by being washed through the cleansing of the Word (Eph. 5:26). Numerous other scriptures give us great hope that we have the heavenly resources to cleanse ourselves.

Glorify God With Your Spirit

So, how can we begin to clean ourselves from the filth this world deposits on us during our daily contending with sin, our flesh, and the devil? We must make it our business to consciously glorify God with our spirits. The text below says we are to glorify God not just with our bodies, although many pastors tend to focus only on that, week after week, in their sermons. Glorifying God involves more than just *behavior modification*; it's also *spirit sanctification*.

> For ye are bought with a price: therefore glorify God in your body, and in your spirit, which are God's.
>
> —1 CORINTHIANS 6:20

When believers choose not to fall for the evil one's traps, which would cause their spirits to dishonor God, their spirits are glorifying God. In another instance the apostle Peter instructed us to "sanctify the Lord God in your hearts" (1 Pet. 3:15). The word *heart* here can be synonymous with the word *spirit*. God won't sanctify our spirits for us; we must choose to do it ourselves by internally saying no to the things the Holy Spirit warns us to stay away from. He will sound the alarm in our consciences—in our spirits—to leave a place, to turn away from a temptation, to run from sin and never look back, lest we taint ourselves with the filthiness of the world. The Book of Isaiah tells us a little more about this external filthiness:

> For all tables are full of vomit and filthiness,
> so that there is no place clean.
>
> —ISAIAH 28:8

Paul told the Corinthian church they couldn't eat at both the table of the Lord and the table of demons (1 Cor. 10:21). Just as your spirit is nourished when you spend time in prayer, fasting, and reading the Word, the opposite is true. If you are feasting at the table of carnality, the flesh, and sin, your spirit (though it is still intact because Christ is living on the inside) is getting more vexed and filthy on the outside, just like Lot was vexed by the sinfulness in the city of Sodom (2 Pet. 2:7–8). Heaven wants you to focus on glorifying God not only in your daily walk but also with your spirit. As the Holy Spirit is monitoring our every thought, I'm sure He is grieved when believers open their spirits to demonic influence and attachment, because that can cause clean spirits to become filthy. For this reason the Holy Spirit will give you an internal indicator when things are starting to affect your spirit. You may begin to experience an uneasy feeling deep inside your spirit that brings conviction to your heart.

Pray to the Father that you never lose the convicting voice of the Holy Spirit, for without it you will lose your ability to know what is truly grieving Him. This is why David prayed in Psalm 51, "Don't take your Holy Spirit from me" (v. 11). The best way to not lose the voice of the Holy Spirit is to always *take heed* and *pay attention* when your spirit is grieved and telling you to stay away from something.

Take Heed of Your Spirit

I wish I had learned the principle of heeding my spirit many years ago. In the early days of my faith I was spiritually lazy, leaving all forms of discernment to the Holy Spirit. Yes, we must always listen to the Holy Spirit's voice and abide by what's written in Scripture, but there are times when we also need to take heed of what our spirits are telling us internally. As a believer your spirit is alive in Christ, and you have relationship with Christ via the spirit, so it's safe to say that your spirit can talk to the rest of you, including your mind.

I have been saved for thirty years, and as I look back, I can clearly remember times my spirit was trying to tell me to stay away from certain people or things. When I was single, at times my spirit would constrain me from putting myself in a compromising position that would cause me to sin. Other times I would be watching a movie, and my spirit would sound the alarm for me to walk out of the room; five minutes later, questionable scenes would play on the screen. I think we all can reflect and remember moments when we didn't heed what our spirits were telling us to do.

> For the LORD, the God of Israel, saith that he hateth putting away: for one covereth violence with his garment, saith the LORD of

hosts: therefore take heed to your spirit, that
ye deal not treacherously.

—MALACHI 2:16

Taking heed to your spirit is an immensely important part of maintaining your deliverance. Think, for example, how this could be connected to divorcing a spouse and covering up sin. God hates divorce. Whatever causes a marriage to end, it's safe to say that the devil and his forces are at work and that one or both parties aren't taking heed to their spirits—the same goes for any sin that can contaminate you.

Disciplining yourself to heed your spirit takes time and effort. You must quiet your spirit, shutting out the busyness of life and the noise of the cares of the world, and *learn to listen* to the Spirit. The great news is that you don't have to do this in your own strength; you can ask the Holy Spirit to help you. But I must caution you: when He offers help in the form of a warning, obey Him. Don't second-guess or simply take a half step. As you feel conviction grip you, whether it's mild or severe, learn to lean into it and follow what the Lord tells you to do—*especially* when He is showing you that your spirit is filthy.

Here are some steps to cleanse yourself of the filth that may be on your spirit. First, *recognize* the conviction of the Holy Spirit pressing on your spirit, which may be trying to communicate that it is filthy or nearing a filthy state. Second, *respond* to that conviction by doing what the Holy Spirit tells you to do. If that means you need to turn off the TV, stop listening to a certain musical artist, stay off the internet late at night—whatever it is, do it. Third, *renew* your spirit by practicing the Christian disciplines that allow your spirit to grow, such as spending time in the Word, worshipping the Lord on a regular basis, and so on. When you do these things daily, you will find your spirit being cleansed, and your need for deliverance sessions will decrease dramatically.

SECRET 6: MAINTAIN YOUR BODY

Once, during a time of deep consecration, I heard the Holy Spirit tell me, "My people have Me held hostage in their hearts, but I want to live in their bodies." What a powerful statement! Prior to that it had never dawned on me that God wanted to be so active in my body, coming to rest on it like He did with the saints in the Old Testament. In those days the Holy Spirit didn't live *inside* anyone, but He rested *upon* those who lived their lives faithfully according to the Law of Moses. That is, the Holy Spirit would rest on an individual, and that person would accomplish great exploits, but once the task was done, the Spirit of God would lift from the person. Thank God for Jesus! He redeemed us and bought us back to God, then deposited the Holy Spirit within us as the "earnest" or guarantee (1. Cor. 10:22). The same Spirit who raised Christ from the dead now lives inside us, according to Romans 8:11.

Throughout my years in deliverance ministry it had never occurred to me that this same Spirit actually wanted to live and rest *on my body*. How do I know this now? Because Luke 13:10–13 talks about a woman with a spirit of infirmity that was crippling her body. Now, I'm not saying that all sicknesses are caused by demonic influence (most are actually the result of sin and bad eating habits), but some are. In the instance of this woman a demon was causing her back to be bent over, and when Jesus set her free, she was able to stand straight again. This lets me know that at times, the devil can lodge in body parts. (I talk about this extensively in my first book, *The Secrets to Deliverance*.) So, it behooves us to live in such a way that even our bodies are completely saturated by the presence of God.

What can we do to prevent our body parts from being given over to sin? Let's look below:

> Do not let any part of your body become an instrument of evil to serve sin. Instead, give yourselves completely to God, for you were dead, but now you have new life. So, use your whole body as an instrument to do what is right for the glory of God.
>
> —ROMANS 6:13, NLT

I know this verse is usually seen in a more metaphorical sense, but it's clear that our bodies can be used as instruments for the enemy. Consider the times when we backbite or gossip about one another. It can get to the point that demons may be lodging right in our mouths, causing us to use them in a way that displeases the Lord. I'm not saying that all negative speech is caused by the devil, but I am saying some Christians have nasty mouths. This is why Paul tells us to allow God to govern our body parts.

Once the Holy Spirit told me He wanted to live on my body, I made it my business to try to seek the Lord in a way that mimicked Moses when he spent forty days in God's presence and afterward literally shone with the glory of God. Now, I know that story is not meant to be prescriptive for us, but I don't think it's necessarily wrong to seek God in that fashion. How could it be? Surely not seeking Him at all and allowing our bodies to remain carnal and lukewarm isn't the answer.

When believers are so filled with God that the devil takes notice, he doesn't try as hard to tempt them, because he sees they have disciplined themselves to be overwhelmed with God's presence in their lives. However, if the devil comes knocking and a believer does get caught up in sin involving the body, God has given us the answer: *Cut it off.*

Gouge It Out

If I could write a whole book on the principle in the following Bible passage, I would, because it's my favorite scripture regarding personal holiness. This principle—the power of *cutting it off*—will help you maintain your spiritual freedom. I wish this version of Christianity was preached more, because the church I know today is so tolerant of compromise, lukewarmness, and carnality that they are feasting at the table with demons and drinking from the devil's cup (1 Cor. 10:21). Nothing removes the devil faster, and then keeps him away better, than gouging something out or cutting it off:

> So if your eye—even your good eye—causes you to lust, gouge it out and throw it away. It is better for you to lose one part of your body than for your whole body to be thrown into hell. And if your hand—even your stronger hand—causes you to sin, cut it off and throw it away. It is better for you to lose one part of your body than for your whole body to be thrown into hell.
>
> —MATTHEW 5:29–30, NLT

Why did Jesus give such drastic instructions in this passage? Because at times the best strategy is a militant one. Your freedom is that important—so important that you might need to cut something or someone off to keep your sanctification. In these verses Jesus is *not* telling you to literally cut your eye out or cut your hand off, but He is saying, "Do whatever you have to do to get rid of the sin in your life." To gouge out one's eye requires a deep commitment—it means that no matter how much it hurts, you realize that the pain is still better than losing your soul.

So, if you have a problem with lust, it might require you to "cut off" your computer by getting rid of it or by having someone help you monitor it and hold you accountable. This level of spiritual surgery is needed to follow Christ. You must surgically remove yourself from the things the kingdom of darkness might offer you, whatever that may be. Anyone who knows me can see I embody this verse and this level of consecration, but why? Because I know myself. My flesh knows how to manipulate me, and if left to my own devices, I would deceive myself into justifying just about any sin in my life.

Because of that, I have embraced a *no-nonsense* version of Christianity that entails militant discipline. As I am one of the leading voices for the deliverance ministry, that responsibility *requires* me to live a life that is above reproach. I cannot need an endless cycle of deliverance sessions for failing to cut off whatever I struggle with. If you want to walk in high levels of the anointing for deliverance—the same level of holiness I personally walk in—then *cut off* and *gouge out* everything that doesn't please God.

Note: I personally don't listen to anything secular, I don't watch many movies, I don't watch TV, and I almost never watch the news. I don't listen to worldly music, and I don't hang around carnal Christians or unbelievers on a social level. I know it might sound like I am a Christian hermit, but I'd rather be safe than sorry. Anyone who knows me knows that my personal freedom in Christ is the most valuable thing to me, and I won't hesitate to gouge anything out of my life, should the Lord require it. I live by one motto: *I ain't going to hell for nobody.* Say it out loud with me: "I'm not going to hell for anybody." It isn't worth it.

Present Your Body

The answer to regulating your body successfully is very simple: to be a pure vessel in which the presence of God can dwell, you must offer your body as a living sacrifice. A *living sacrifice* entails everything described in Jesus' words in Matthew 5 above, but it goes a little deeper. Not all sacrifices are blood sacrifices that require a knife. Some sacrifices in the Old Testament were burnt offerings, in which the entire animal was offered on the altar and completely consumed. *Demons cannot enter a sacrifice that is consumed on the altar.* If you give your body completely to the presence of God, the demons will be forced to flee.

> I beseech you therefore, brethren, by the mercies of God, that ye present your bodies a living sacrifice, holy, acceptable unto God, which is your reasonable service.
>
> —ROMANS 12:1

I truly believe that, more than anything, violating this verse causes Christians to lose their freedom. So much emphasis is put on guarding our hearts and minds (which we will cover next), but no real emphasis is put on guarding *our bodies* and offering them to God.

Both Moses and Elijah gave their bodies to God's presence, as did Enoch to the presence of YHWH. And the early church gave their bodies to God's presence so thoroughly that even the Pharisees noticed they had been with Jesus—it was that obvious. So many Christians are pure in their hearts but hateful in how they use their bodies. Make it your personal goal to follow the Holy Spirit's conviction as you offer up your body to His presence.

SECRET 7: MAINTAIN YOUR MIND

I didn't place this secret first because I think most believers know they must guard their minds from the world, the flesh, and the devil. The Bible tells us to guard the heart, which also means "mind," because out of it flows the issues of life (Prov. 4:23). I don't want to regurgitate what others have said in other resources, so let's look at three different things, and you will know what you need to do from there.

The Spirit of Your Mind

The following view is less frequently talked about, but I have found it to be the key in keeping one's mind closed to the demonic. Consider this Scripture passage:

> That ye put off concerning the former conversation the old man, which is corrupt

according to the deceitful lusts; and be renewed in the spirit of your mind.

—EPHESIANS 4:22–23

The "spirit of your mind" can refer to your mind's predisposition and attitude, or your state of mind. Oh man, do demons dwell in our attitudes or states of mind. Have you ever tried to deal with a person whose attitude is deeply pessimistic? (I have noticed that many church people have a pessimistic outlook.) It's almost impossible to change that person's mind to focus on anything positive. Demons dwell in many such deeply poor attitudes. This is why Paul told the believers in Ephesus to allow the Spirit of God to change their attitudes.

Your state of mind needs to be renewed, remade, even created brand-new in some cases. I know exactly what this means, as I was sentenced to nine years in prison as a young person and my outlook in life became deeply flawed as a result of the time I spent incarcerated. I'm surprised my wife even remained married to me because I was an extremely angry man, and my spirit was broken.

Many people who follow deliverance ministries

need to be reminded of the above scripture, because often their minds are so dependent on darkness that they have become overly demon-conscious. (We will deal with this in the next chapter.) The ministry of deliverance is not about fighting the darkness but about turning on the light. So many people seeking deliverance have cast demons out of their minds but not out of their attitudes. Let me be the first to say that not all bad attitudes are demonic, but a bad attitude *will* open the door to the demonic if it is not crucified.

When you renew the spirit of your mind, your attitude will be renewed by the Word, and you will gain a more positive outlook from the Scriptures. Then the demons of negativity will have no place from which to launch an attack. You will not overblame the devil when things don't go your way but will remain optimistic, trusting in the Word, and if need be, you will verbally rebuke the devil, telling him to go back to hell where he came from.

Casting Down Imaginations

When our attitudes have been renewed, we will fight back by casting down all thoughts that come from the enemy:

Casting down imaginations, and every high thing that exalteth itself against the knowledge of God, and bringing into captivity every thought to the obedience of Christ; and having in a readiness to revenge all disobedience, when your obedience is fulfilled.

—2 CORINTHIANS 10:5–6

There is no way to ignore this verse: if you won't control your thought life, the Holy Spirit won't either. You must do your part, taking the initiative to analyze all thoughts that enter your mind. This may take some time to learn, as we are not accustomed to examining what we have been thinking about, but it's possible. *All thoughts* that are from the enemy need to be cast down, with quick vengeance. You can't stop thoughts from entering your head, but you can stop them from remaining there.

Demons dwell in lies; lies in your mind become strongholds; and strongholds, if left unchecked, will become a strongman. Bringing every thought into captivity means that you must arrest everything that enters your mind and line it up with Scripture. Note: *Taking our thoughts captive doesn't mean blanking out our minds.* It means lining up our thoughts with the Word of God. If a thought doesn't measure up to what God's Word says, we reject it and cut it out of our heads.

The kingdom of darkness knows that the best way to enter your body is through your thoughts, for the battlefield is in the mind. In the early days of my Christian experience the battle for my mind was so intense that I would curl up on the floor in the corner of a room and just cry. (I didn't know anything about spiritual warfare and deliverance at that time.) It took me years to learn this principle, but once I did, I became fierce at controlling my thoughts.

Think on These Things

What does "casting down" one's thoughts really look like in practice? Well, as I said, it is not leaving your mind empty after removing all your thoughts. It means removing any thoughts that don't line up with God's Word and replacing them with Scripture, with the things of God, with things that are wholesome and good. You don't necessarily have to spend all day meditating on the Scriptures, although that might be a good start. The apostle Paul told us we can allow other things to come into our minds—our thoughts don't *always* have to be related to something spiritual, but they do need to be positive and not contrary to God's nature and His Word:

> And now, dear brothers and sisters, one final thing. Fix your thoughts on what is true, and honorable, and right, and pure, and lovely, and admirable. Think about things that are excellent and worthy of praise.
> —Philippians 4:8, nlt

In this verse Paul gave us a pretty good blueprint for how to make sure our thoughts don't wander off and inadvertently open the door to the demonic. The best way to do this is to fix our thoughts on what is true and honorable. I won't take time to break down every description in this verse of things with which we should fill our minds; instead, I'm going to give you the opportunity to do that.

Fill in the following blanks by looking up the meaning of each italicized word and writing it in the space provided. By the time you finish, the definition of each word will be embedded in your heart and mind, and you will have a good starting place for replacing any ungodly thoughts with positive, godly ones.

1. What is *true*?

_____

2. What is *honorable*?

_____

3. What is *right*?

_____

4. What is *pure*?

_____

5. What is *lovely*?

_____

6. What is *admirable*?

_____

As you write out these definitions, pray the following prayer:

> *Heavenly Father, I thank You for giving me Your Word so that I can meditate on the things that honor You and keep my mind in perfect peace. I command any unclean spirits still lingering in my mind to leave me now, in Jesus' name. I bind all your activity in my thoughts, and I declare that I have the mind of Christ. Lord Jesus, thank You for helping me take every thought captive to You and aligning it with Your Word. I declare my mind to be free from any distractions, any high thing that exalts itself against You. My mind is clear, my mind is free, my mind is pure, and my mind dwells on things that please You. In Jesus' name, amen.*

Secret 8: Maintain Your Soul

The soul is the seat of our emotions. This is why maintaining our souls is crucial. The way we feel is a large contributor to the ways in which we act. Because of this the Bible tells us many times to allow the Word of God and the Holy Spirit to govern our emotions. Unhealthy emotions can lead to irreversible actions. This is what happened to Cain; the Bible says he felt "angry" and "dejected" because God wasn't pleased with his offering (Gen. 4:5, NLT), and eventually those feelings led to the murder of his brother Abel.

If the Holy Spirit can get us to crucify our feelings and allow our souls to be healed, we will become mature in our thinking and will not be swayed to and fro, like a wave of the sea.

We are emotional beings. God made us to have feelings and express those feelings to each other. Most of modern civilization is governed and dominated by feelings—reaction is the currency of the day. Almost everything we do is centered around our feelings and emotions. I wish it wasn't like this, but it's true. We react to things more emotionally than logically. The demons know this, and worse, they know which buttons to push to cause even believers to get into their feelings.

God gave us feelings to enjoy the beauty and joy of life, but our modern civilization—especially what happens online—loves to exploit them. Social media is the new gladiator arena, as people slaughter each other with their words just to get a reaction. Our reactions are now even monetized, which is why this next passage is so important. Let's read:

> Be ye angry, and sin not: let not the sun go down upon your wrath: Neither give place to the devil.
>
> —Ephesians 4:26–27

These verses are often used to gain an understanding of the demonic, and rightly so, but that's not the only point to Paul's words here. If you pay close attention, you can spot the emotion that is inseparable from the truth of this scripture. This emotion has been around since the beginning of recorded civilization. Most of us look at these verses and focus on not giving place to the devil, but I look at this passage for its *emotional* truth. Verse 26 says to "let not the sun go down upon your wrath." Wrath is an emotion. It takes place when anger hasn't been properly dealt with and processed. When people reach the point of wrath, the only thing left for them to do is to express their anger in a destructive manner.

This is why our emotions need to be regulated

with Scripture and prayer—especially prayer. God is not saying that we should not experience emotions. The text says it's OK to get angry—*for the right reason*—but we are not to allow that anger to cross over into wrath. Wrath is what caused Cain to kill his brother.

The Word tells us not to sin because of our anger—which means that our emotions can lead us to sin. However, a believer can "redeem the time" spent in a negative emotion by working through it. An example of this is social media; take some time off from social media platforms when you know tensions are high in your life or in society in general. For instance, as we have seen in the last several elections, social media can become a bloodbath of disagreements concerning who should be elected to the presidency. This is why I have personally chosen to turn off comments on my timeline; it protects my emotions and keeps me from getting angry as the immaturity of people (including believers) causes them to verbally and violently attack each other online. I refuse to give place to the devil—and so should you.

I will keep my soul in perfect harmony, filled

with God's peace. I will not allow my emotions to become the devil's playground. My thoughts should not become an amusement park for the demonic, in which they ride the roller coaster of my feelings. The devil is a liar. Say it out loud with me right now: *The devil is a liar.*

SECRET 9: MAINTAIN YOUR MOUTH

Without sensationalizing the power of our words, we can agree that what we say has a direct effect on the world around us. The Bible says that the world we now see was framed by God's words. The principle is that words have *creative power* to cause our environment to be filled with either joy or chaos. This is why the Bible speaks consistently about watching our words.

No Corrupt Communication

This secret is somewhat more important than others in that, without its implementation, the results can be deadly. As I mentioned before, your spirit can't be corrupted because you and Christ are one, but your mouth isn't one with Christ—at least this side of heaven. So, yes, your mouth can become corrupted. The Bible even says the words of your mouth can corrupt your whole body. So, it's crucial that you understand this key secret to maintaining your deliverance.

Let me start by saying this, which you may have heard someone say to you in your childhood: *shut your mouth*. Why did I say that? Because your mouth is likely getting you in more trouble than your mind and emotions put together. So many things are ruined by our words. The Bible says that by your words you will be either justified or condemned (Matt. 12:37). Again, unlike your spirit, your mouth can be corrupted. Even true, authentic believers can corrupt their mouths by failing to heed the following scripture:

> Let no corrupt communication proceed out
> of your mouth, but that which is good to the
> use of edifying, that it may minister grace
> unto the hearers.
>
> —EPHESIANS 4:29

If you fail to use your mouth to edify and instead use it in ways that make the demons happy, your mouth will slowly start corrupting itself. Something corrupts itself when, within its nature, it slowly breaks itself down. One thing about corruption is that it's internal and very slow; it's never a quick process—and if there is one thing demons have on their hands, it is *time*. Demons are patient. They have been around for thousands of years, and they know which buttons to push to get you to sin with your mouth. They know that if they can get a believer to agree with their lies and confess them with the mouth, it is more than likely those words will cause the person to stumble. As the Bible says, you will the eat the fruit of your words (Prov. 18:21).

I can honestly say I have finally learned to control my words, but it has taken years. This is not an area where I typically struggle, but I have seen how hell itself has used believers' words to destroy relationships, families, and even churches. Slander is at an all-time high in our society today; so is corrupt speech. Negative words are more commonly spoken than anything positive, and demons are behind most of it. You might be saying, "Pagani is exaggerating about this," but the next verse will confirm that hell has a social connection to your words.

The Power of the Tongue

> Among all the parts of the body, the tongue is a flame of fire. It is a whole world of wickedness, corrupting your entire body. It can set your whole life on fire, for it is set on fire by hell itself.
>
> —James 3:6, NLT

When I read the last part of that verse, it blew me away: our tongues are "set on fire by hell itself." Wow! What a mind-blowing verse. As clear and plain as day, right here in the Book of James, the Scripture is telling you that *hell's greatest weapon is your tongue*. This is why the devil is so eager to control it.

One quick way to lose your deliverance is to confess with your mouth the lie that "deliverance didn't work because I don't feel any different." Deliverance is not a feeling—it's a legal exchange. If you are certain that you followed through with all the steps in your deliverance session, then *just know* that it worked. Give it some time, and you will begin to see the changes take place. But if you start getting negative and begin to confess the devil's lies that he places in your head, or if you fail to quote scripture like Jesus did in the wilderness of temptation (Matt. 4), then you can expect the effects of your words to begin to happen.

Allow the truth of James 3:6 to really sink in. To be honest, I just received the revelation of this verse not many years ago—and I've been a Christian since 1994. I wish I had learned this sooner because I would not have taken so much loss from the devil through my words. All of James 3 is dedicated to talking about our mouths and the power of the tongue. My assignment for you right now is to read that entire chapter before you continue reading any further in this book.

SECRET 10: MAINTAIN YOUR EARS

Let's look at the secret of maintaining our ears from a different angle rather than from the approach most people take. When I understood the following revelation about guarding my ears, the success I had in spiritual warfare moved to a whole new level.

Uncircumcised Ears

The covenant practice of circumcision involves the act of "cutting away." Eight days after a Hebrew boy was born, according to the Old Testament law, the parents were to have the child circumcised. This involved the cutting away of the male foreskin as a physical demonstration that the Israelite people were in covenant with the God of Abraham. This ritual was a painful one, but it was required to maintain a literal distinction between the children of Israel and the pagan nations who did not honor God. With that in mind, let's look at the following verse and glean insights from it:

> Ye stiff-necked and uncircumcised in heart
> and ears, ye do always resist the Holy Ghost:
> as your fathers did, so do ye.
>
> —ACTS 7:51

How does this accusation apply to believers, especially in regard to keeping themselves from being put into bondage again? The answer is that some believers continue to listen to things that do not please God or edify their growth. This verse alludes to the predisposition of one's ears being *cut away* (that is, circumcised). When your ear is circumcised from the things of the world, of the flesh, and of the kingdom of darkness, being disciplined in what you listen to becomes extremely easy.

> You were dead because of your sins and because your sinful nature was not yet cut away. Then God made you alive with Christ, for he forgave all our sins. He canceled the record of the charges against us and took it away by nailing it to the cross. In this way, he disarmed the spiritual rulers and authorities. He shamed them publicly by his victory over them on the cross.
>
> —Colossians 2:13–15, nlt

When the natural, sinful tendencies of your ears have been "cut away" by your obedience to Scripture, the devil can't come through your ear gates anymore. That opening is closed off to him. In Acts 7 Stephen told the Jewish leaders that their ears and their hearts were uncircumcised and that the result was stubbornness. If you're having a hard time with stubbornness in your life, there's a good chance that your struggle is with your ears and what you're listening to. Ask God to circumcise your ears, and see if your stubbornness goes away. If you don't allow the Word to circumcise your ears, then ultimately you will end up resisting the Holy Spirit and straying from sound doctrine.

Itching Ears

Many in the deliverance movement want to be free but don't have freedom because they don't place a high value on Scripture. Upholding sound doctrine is extremely important, but why? In the Book of 1 Timothy we are told that many will leave sound doctrine, "giving heed to seducing spirits, and doctrines of devils" (4:1). The connection between false doctrine and the demonic realm is clear.

> For a time is coming when people will no longer listen to sound and wholesome teaching. They will follow their own desires and will look for teachers who will tell them whatever their itching ears want to hear. They will reject the truth and chase after myths.
>
> —2 TIMOTHY 4:3–4, NLT

Having "itching ears" refers to seeking out messages and doctrines that condone one's own lifestyle, as opposed to adhering to the teachings of Scripture. When a group of people starts to move away from sound doctrine, it always opens the door to the demonic. The more truth believers stray away from, the more lies they will embrace; and the more lies they embrace, the more the potential for demonic activity will increase.

This is why dealing with "itching ears" is a crucial part of this secret to maintain your deliverance. If you don't, the devil may cause you to stray into error, and nothing causes a believer to go in circles more than faulty theology. When your theology is wrong, your beliefs will be wrong. And when your beliefs are wrong, your life will very quickly go wrong. I wish more deliverance ministries of today would place as high of a value on Scripture as they do on identifying demons.

Demons love to get believers offtrack on the road of myth rather than truth. In the early days of my deliverance ministry I, too, held some erroneous beliefs. They didn't move into the realm of false doctrine, but they were definitely in error, and they caused me a lot of heartache. Thank God the Holy Spirit was able to snatch me up before I began to teach those things—or even fully believe them. Thank God for the truth!

Note: deliverance is not a power encounter but a *truth* encounter. As Jesus said, "Ye shall know the truth, and the truth shall make you free" (John 8:32).

Tune Your Ears

What is the solution to making sure you don't stray into error? The answer is to *tune your ears.*

> Tune your ears to wisdom, and concentrate on understanding.
> —PROVERBS 2:2, NLT

I love the word *tune* here, because it makes me think of fine-tuning a stringed instrument, which can be done only by *closely listening* to it. When tuning a guitar, for example, the musician has to get close to the strings, playing each note and then turning the tuning knobs appropriately until the proper sound comes from the instrument. In the same way, we must tune our ears.

The NLT's wording of this proverb from King Solomon (who some say was the wisest person to ever live) implies that our ears can be out of tune. A personal saying I have lived by since I first became a Christian is this: "Tell me the truth even if I don't like it." In the Psalms, King David often wrote things like "Lead me in thy truth, and teach me" (25:5) and "His truth shall be thy shield and buckler" (91:4). That depth of love for the truth can be attained only when a person fine-tunes his ears to listen closely to it.

SECRET 11: MAINTAIN YOUR EYES

As we close out this chapter, let's look at one verse that I personally live by and that has been a safeguard, protecting me from the onslaught of evil that the TV and the internet have to offer. I can say with a clear conscience that personally, I don't struggle with pornography, a wandering eye, or "the lust of the eyes" (1 John 2:16). Why has this become a nonissue for me? Because I made a covenant with my eyes. Just like the ears need to be circumcised, the eyes also need to come into covenant with the Lord. This powerful verse should be committed to memory and put into practice by every believer, especially those in ministry:

> I made a covenant with mine eyes; why then should I think upon a maid?
>
> —JOB 31:1

The word *covenant* in Hebrew means "agreement, pledge"[3] and may involve the parties exchanging items to solidify their agreement.[4] Most Christians will turn to prayer concerning the discipline of their eyes (and there is nothing wrong with that), but this verse implies in a metaphoric sense that *you must enter this covenant by choice.* To better understand how this is accomplished, consider the apostle Paul, who said, "I buffet my body and put it under subjection." (See 1 Corinthians 9:27.) This is something you need to do with the help of the Holy Spirit. If you won't do it, God won't do it.

With the Holy Spirit's help you must make the willful choice to set up terms of agreement concerning what you will or won't watch. I did this back in 2014. During a season of fasting, I walked into the kitchen one day and heard a voice speak to my heart, "Do you want to experience more of God's presence?"

My quick response was "Yes, Lord."

I then heard Him say, "Go to the living room, and delete all the recorded TV shows on your DVR, all the mafia and prison movies." At that point it had never dawned on me that heaven wasn't pleased with me watching those movies. I'd always loved a good mafia movie. But heaven was now requiring me to give those things up.

I got on my knees and gave up those kinds of movies that day, and I have never watched them again. I also made a vow never to watch TV again—and I have kept that vow to this very day.

When God told me I was "the Pagani everyone knows and loves," I was actually just a simple pastor of a church in the Bronx, New York City, who was just getting the hang of deliverance ministry. But once I made a covenant with my eyes to no longer watch those movies and TV shows, within a few short months I had been invited to speak about deliverance on TBN, then The Word Network, and then other Christian television networks; Charisma House offered me a book deal, and I ended up traveling all over the world sharing about the deliverance ministry.

Don't get me wrong: I'm not talking about being legalistic with your eyes. Rather, I'm referring to making a covenant with your eyes, an internal agreement in which you tell God that you will no longer watch the things that displease Him. As your eyes remain pure in His sight, in return God will honor His covenant and bless you.

I want you to make a covenant with your eyes and write it out below. That is how we are going to close this chapter.

> *Heavenly Father, I make a covenant with my eyes to never watch* [write what you're never going to watch again].

_____

_____

_____

_____

> *With the help of the Holy Spirit, I will honor this covenant, written by my own hand. May heaven acknowledge the terms of this covenant, in Jesus' name. Amen.*

CHAPTER 4

THE SECRETS OF MANDATORY AVOIDANCE

> When you go to war against your enemies, be sure to *stay away* from anything that is impure.
>
> —DEUTERONOMY 23:9, NLT
> EMPHASIS ADDED

> If a bird sees a trap being set, it knows to *stay away*. But these people set an ambush for themselves.
>
> —PROVERBS 1:17–18, NLT
> EMPHASIS ADDED

> Wherefore come out from among them, and be ye separate, says the Lord, and *touch not* the unclean thing; and I will receive you.
>
> —2 CORINTHIANS 6:17
> EMPHASIS ADDED

JUST LIKE A user guide tells you how a product works, it also includes sections that inform you how *not* to use the product. Using the product in a manner that the manufacturer didn't intend is problematic because it could cause the product to malfunction.

Note: *you have no right to say that deliverance doesn't work if you approach it irresponsibly.* If you violate the laws of liberty, then you can't expect to remain set free.

The Bible says that liberty is a law—which means there is a system of rules and regulations to protect it, enforce it, and keep it operational.

> But whoso looketh into the perfect *law of liberty*, and continueth therein, he being not a forgetful hearer, but a doer of the work, this man shall be blessed in his deed.
>
> —JAMES 1:25
> EMPHASIS ADDED

Notice that this verse doesn't say "promise of liberty"; it says "law of liberty." Many people who need and want deliverance view it through a relational lens, relying on a "promise" to be set free. They don't realize that their freedom is actually legislative, not relational. So, if they sit idly by, waiting for a promise to come to pass, a misguided sense of entitlement can set in. Then when deliverance is nowhere to be found, they become angry and frustrated and even entertain feelings of rejection.

There are rules of engagement involved in maintaining your liberty. The phrase *rules of engagement* refers to a set of orders or guidelines that establish what can and cannot be done during an armed conflict. In Deuteronomy 23:9, the opening verse to this chapter, we read how the Lord told the children of Israel to "*stay away* from anything that is impure" during times of warfare (NLT, emphasis added). Why? Because you can't wage a successful warfare campaign against the enemy if you are violating the rules of engagement—it will be a guaranteed loss.

The goal of all those who experience deliverance is to maintain it, not lose it. But the quickest way to lose your deliverance is to violate the rules of engagement.

Your liberty has laws that must be obeyed. These laws are *perfect*—they work if you work them. They will protect you if you enforce them, but they will also malfunction if you violate them. I believe this is why James 1:25 uses the word *law* instead of *promise*; if a law is involved, we need to know what the violations are so we can *stay away* from them.

So, in this chapter we will focus on the secrets of "staying away." I'm going to outline and define some things from which you should stay away—things I have learned through personal experience or violations I have seen others commit throughout the years that can cause people to lose their deliverance after only a short period of time.

It breaks my heart to see so many believers walking in defeat, even after undergoing multiple deliverance sessions. This doesn't have to be the norm. You can be free and *stay free*, but you must make it your business to follow the rules of engagement and learn to stay away from reopening those doors by not being ignorant of Satan's devices.

> Lest Satan should get an advantage of us: for we are not ignorant of his devices.
> —2 CORINTHIANS 2:11

Many of the devices I'll list are things many believers just aren't aware of. This list is not exhaustive, and it's not in any particular order, but it is a good set of rules to abide by. It will help safeguard you from losing any ground gained through your deliverance.

I feel impressed by the Lord that before we continue this chapter and look at the next group of secrets, it's imperative to stress one important fact.

NOT EVERYTHING IS A DEMON

Everything ain't a demon. I know that's not proper grammar, but I'm speaking as a New Yorker from the Bronx when I say this. I wish I could write a book with that very title, because it needs to be said—loudly—in every deliverance circle all over the world. I'm not sure why this statement causes a stir among so many in the deliverance camp. (I guess it's because they're so used to the church never blaming the devil for anything.) Still, more teaching needs to be given on this because it's true.

I'm being completely honest when I say that a vast majority of the people who come to our ministry for deliverance *don't actually have a demon—* but they think they do, and trust me when I tell you, it's hard to convince them otherwise. We end up praying for them regardless, and as I take the time to really talk with these people, I realize that the symptoms they think are caused by a demon often can be diagnosed as a mental or emotional problem or some other issue that doesn't require a deliverance session.

Now, I'm not saying that some problems *aren't* the result of a demon—I wrote two best-selling books on the demonic realm, so I'm not minimizing the problems that demons do cause. But many of the issues people experience aren't caused by demons. Because of that, before we move on, I want you to say this out loud: "Everything ain't a demon." Sometimes it's the world, the flesh, or the devil just looking to choke out the Word we're carrying inside our hearts.

> For everything in the world—the lust of the flesh, the lust of the eyes, and the pride of life—comes not from the Father but from the world.
>
> —1 JOHN 2:16, NIV

So, now let's look at the next group of secrets. Some will include biblical references to help explain them, and others simply come from advice I can give from years of experience in the deliverance ministry.

Secret 12: Stay Away From Legalism and Perfectionism

Legalism is a dangerous virus to the deliverance ministry. That's because the law has no room for compassion or faith, and deliverance is a ministry of faith activated by love. The law is overly critical and demands perfection. The law brings condemnation, which works against your remaining in faith after a deliverance session. Condemnation will cause you to assume that you weren't actually delivered or to fiercely criticize yourself for any mistake you make after the session.

My personal battle against legalism has caused me to fight against the temptation toward perfectionism, beginning with my first deliverance session. After that session if I made the slightest mistake or got angry for any reason, my first thought was "I wasn't truly set free," and I went into behavior modification, trying to remove the overwhelming feelings of false guilt.

Just know this: After your deliverance you will make many mistakes as you learn to obey Scripture and establish new habits. It will take time (sometimes a *long* time) to learn to walk in this newfound freedom. Learn to give yourself room to make mistakes and stay away from perfectionism. *You will not suddenly be perfect after your deliverance.*

Am I telling you to not set up rules and regulations or establish boundaries? No. Rules are good, but legalism is bad. There is a difference between guidelines that leave room for error and legalistic rules that bring only condemnation. The apostle Paul dealt with this with the church in Colossae. Read below:

> You have died with Christ, and he has set you free from the spiritual powers of this world. So why do you keep on following the rules of the world, such as, "Don't handle! Don't taste! Don't touch!"? Such rules are mere human teachings about things that deteriorate as we use them.
> —Colossians 2:20–22, nlt

There is only one way to make sure you don't fall into the trap of legalism and perfectionism, and that is to *be dead to it.* You will find that the revelation of "being dead" comes up quite frequently in Paul's writings. The understanding is this: Something can't affect you if you're dead to it.

It took me some time to really allow this scripture to sink into my heart and render myself dead to legalism. Once I did a word study on this concept of being dead, I made it my business to walk in it. Oh my Lord, was it hard to break free from perfectionism. But I learned to make room for my errors after my deliverance. Whenever I made a mistake, I simply asked God to forgive me and moved on.

Give yourself room to make mistakes as you learn to walk in your freedom. *Ask God to forgive you,* and then simply move on.

SECRET 13: STAY AWAY FROM SUPERSTITION

Superstition seems to be a growing trend in many deliverance circles. What is superstition? It is "a widely held but unjustified belief in supernatural causation leading to certain consequences of an action or event, or a practice based on such a belief."[1] In a nutshell—what we can't explain we blame. When things go wrong or weird occurrences cause us concern, we tend to blame demons, or we start to develop odd beliefs that have no validity. In our minds we are so sure that whatever is happening is caused by a demon.

> Paul stood in the midst of Mars' hill, and said, Ye men of Athens, I perceive that in all things ye are too *superstitious*. For as I passed by, and beheld your devotions, I found an altar with this inscription, TO THE UNKNOWN GOD. Whom therefore ye ignorantly worship, him declare I unto you."
> —ACTS 17:22–23
> EMPHASIS ADDED

In our newfound freedom we start to develop the superstitious mindset of the people of Athens. What do I mean? In our quest to stay free, we tend to become superstitious with everything around us, and we fear that anything we can't explain is some counterattack to our deliverance or demons trying to reenter our bodies. Let me be the first to tell you this: *Not everything that remains unexplained after your deliverance is a demon. Sometimes it's just life.*

SECRET 14: STAY AWAY FROM SEEKING ATTENTION

I don't think most believers intend to seek attention, but many do. They come to deliverance sessions not because they really want to be set free but because it allows them to gain some sort of attention from the church or the deliverance ministers.

> Don't call attention to yourself; let others do
> that for you.
>
> —PROVERBS 27:2, MSG

Sometimes it baffles me how many times I've seen the opposite of this verse in operation. Countless hours and sessions are spent trying to help someone get free from demonic contamination, only to learn that the person has become obsessed with deliverance because it combats the loneliness he or she feels. This verse tells us not to call attention to ourselves but to allow the Lord to place it on others' hearts and minds to seek us out.

At times this need for attention can become a distraction, such as when a person is exaggerating a manifestation by overly screaming and crying during a session. Multiple deliverance workers have to restrain the person, even when it's obviously not a true demonic manifestation.

Stay away from this level of attention-seeking behavior. Most deliverance sessions are quiet, orderly, and organized (not all, but a lot). Deliverance is actually a legal exchange, and demons will have to leave when you fulfill all the requirements to secure your freedom.

Ask yourself, "Am I seeking attention, or am I truly seeking to be set free?"

SECRET 15: STAY AWAY FROM BEING DEMON-CONSCIOUS

I know you've heard it said that some people see "a demon under every rock" (which refers to those who look for or see a demon in everything that happens). Throughout the years I've heard many churches and believers use that phrase, and at first it baffled me because where I came from, nobody ever blamed the devil for anything. Everything was a result of either the flesh, the world, or some other reason. I remember thinking, "Where is this crowd who overblames the devil?" Up to that point I had never seen them. But not too long after that, God began to bless our ministry to travel, and little by little this crowd began to emerge from the caves. This group of saints do, in fact, tend to see the demonic in everything—from coffee to hand gestures, to street signs and symbols on or in buildings (which can be occultic), to cell phones and 5G towers. To them every sickness has a direct line to hell. I have to laugh, because we know this is not true, but people in this crowd have become so demon-conscious that they have lost the beauty of seeing where God is working.

The Bible says, "The earth is the Lord's, and the fulness thereof" (Ps. 24:1). Yes, the devil is at work through "the children of disobedience" (Eph. 2:2), but God is *more* at work than the devil. Deliverance is a matter not of fighting the darkness but of turning on the light.

> Ye are all the children of light, and the children of the day: we are not of the night, nor of darkness.
>
> —1 THESSALONIANS 5:5

This is hard for so many of us who are accustomed to seeing more darkness because of the way we grew up and the culture in which we've been raised. But I assure you that such line of thinking doesn't please God. I was guilty, in my early years of deliverance ministry, of being extremely focused on the darkness, but that is why I'm writing this book: to provide a *balanced* view of the demonic realm.

I encourage you to stay away from becoming so focused on the devil that you see more darkness than light. Remember what we learned in chapter 1: We are children of the light, and our armor is light. The Word is light, and the Holy Spirit illuminates it for us. All this should cause our subconscious to be more centered on seeing what heaven is doing and where heaven is than where the devil is operating.

Are you overly demon-conscious? Then you're already giving the kingdom of darkness more and more ground because you're not walking as a child of the light. Repent right now, and ask the Lord to keep you focused on a well-balanced view of the demonic rather than going to extremes and spotting the devil under every rock.

SECRET 16: STAY AWAY FROM IRRESPONSIBILITY

God won't do for you what He requires you to do yourself. You can ask for His strength to help you in fulfilling your responsibilities, but ultimately *you* must do it. If you want lasting freedom, you must do the work: you must take control of your mind, must turn down the food plate in a fasting time, must resist the devil, must shut your eyes to lust, and must spend time feasting on the Scriptures. If you won't, then God won't. The Lord has granted you the weapons of warfare to help, but if you won't take responsibility to use them, the Bible calls that sin.

> Remember, it is sin to know what you ought
> to do and then not do it.
>
> —JAMES 4:17, NLT

I know we are not used to viewing irresponsibility as actual sin, but it is. Yes, irresponsibility opens the door to the demonic. The Book of James tells us that if we fail to do what is right, that is sin, and sin opens the door to demons. I have been able to maintain my deliverance for long periods of time because I know what I need to do, and I'm responsible with my freedom. Be responsible with *your* freedom.

This area is where most pastors remain frustrated with the ministry of deliverance, because many of those who receive freedom fail to take any responsibility afterward to maintain it. Pastors spend more time cleaning up messes from deliverance ministry than from any other ministry. As of this year I have spent twenty years serving as the lead pastor of a church, and I've found that on numerous occasions the answer to a person's freedom was nothing more than having him or her take responsibility to keep the door closed to the devil.

SECRET 17: STAY AWAY FROM CULTISH RITUALS

I write these words with deep frustration today, because I just learned that a three-year-old girl in Northern California died at the hands of her mom, grandfather (a pastor), and uncle as they attempted to perform an exorcism on her. In their ignorance they turned to cultish rituals and assumed that deliverance must involve vomiting. Multiple times they pried her mouth open and put their fingers down her throat, trying to cause her to vomit to get what they thought was a demon to come out.[2]

Deliverance does not equal vomiting. Do demons at times come out through vomiting? Yes, but vomiting is not a mandatory ritual that must be followed.

All three adults involved in this case have been charged with child abuse resulting in death.[3] Yet I think that if we don't teach the church how to operate in biblical deliverance, this will be only the beginning. Through the years I have seen some bizarre rituals take place in church services, with the minister claiming it was "spiritual warfare." I remember that in 1995, one preacher would get up in the middle of services and just start screaming at the devil at the top of his lungs, binding and loosing. One time he was so disruptive that security was called and he was escorted out of the building. I have so many stories about these weird practices. But one thing I know is that those who perform or are recipients of such rituals almost instantly lose their freedom after it is achieved.

Stay away from these extreme, bizarre rituals that pose as valid deliverance tactics. Ask yourself whether they glorify Christ or steer attention away from Christ and onto the practices themselves. Some rituals in the church are beautiful, such as water baptism, Communion, and even foot washing; these are sanctioned by Jesus because they serve as symbols of Christ and His work. However, many of the strange deliverance rituals we see lean more toward witchcraft and occult practices.

SECRET 18: STAY AWAY FROM ASSUMPTIONS

What is an *assumption*? It is "a thing that is accepted as true or as certain to happen, without proof."[4] Since most people who receive deliverance are new to this type of ministry, they come with many preconceived ideas that are not based on truth or Scripture. Because they haven't taken the time to understand how deliverance works and because not many deliverance ministries have a solid follow-up system, those who receive deliverance are left to figure out what happens next, including how to manage their newfound freedom, and it almost always leads to assumptions.

> Fools base their thoughts on foolish assumptions, so their conclusions will be wicked madness.
>
> —ECCLESIASTES 10:13, NLT

When nothing is explained thoroughly after their deliverance, recipients make assumptions about what *they think* is happening. Assumptions lead to misdiagnoses. If we misdiagnose what is occurring, we waste time going down rabbit trails that lead to dead ends. A simple headache is assumed to be caused by a demon. Having a hard time staying focused while reading the Word is attributed to demonic oppression rather than to just being tired after a long day at work.

Sometimes I have to laugh when believers assume various occurrences are demonic even though they can be so easily explained. It truly makes us into fools.

SECRET 19: STAY AWAY FROM UNBELIEF

Let me ask you this: Was your deliverance experience real? Did you witness the power of God remove demons from your life? If so—and you know it— then stay away from anyone or anything that would make you doubt it. It's not a sin to doubt; we all have them. But doubt that isn't crucified with the Word of God will eventually produce unbelief.

> "'If you can'?" said Jesus. "Everything is possible for one who believes." Immediately the boy's father exclaimed, "I do believe; help me overcome my unbelief!"
> —MARK 9:23–24, NIV

This is why it is so crucial that immediately after your deliverance, you take some time to get in the Scriptures and feast on the Word of God. Do a word study on *demons, deliverance,* and the *devil,* and learn everything you can about how Jesus dealt with the demonic realm. Why is this important? Because the Bible says that "faith comes by hearing, and hearing by the word of God" (Rom. 10:17, NKJV).

Again, it's not a sin to have doubts. The passage from Mark expresses the heart's cry of a father whose son had a demon that caused the child to suffer with epileptic seizures. Let me provide some context: Jesus had taken three disciples up a mountain to have an encounter with Moses and Elijah. While they were gone, the nine apostles left at the foot of the mountain were asked to face off with the demon that was possessing this child. Unfortunately they couldn't cast it out, and the father became frustrated. When Jesus arrived, the father approached Him. Jesus asked about the history of the child and then cast the demon out (Matt. 17:1–18; Mark 9:2–27; Luke 9:28–42). Later that night the disciples asked Him why they couldn't cast it out themselves, and He plainly replied:

> Because of your unbelief: for verily I say unto you, If ye have faith as a grain of mustard seed, ye shall say unto this mountain, Remove hence to yonder place; and it shall remove; and nothing shall be impossible unto you.
>
> —MATTHEW 17:20

As you can see, unbelief was the weapon the demon used against the nine apostles. Doubt and unbelief are the devil's playground. If you *know* that your deliverance experience was real, then don't allow anyone (including yourself) or anything else to cause you to doubt it. Stand firm in your faith, knowing that he whom the Son sets free is free indeed.

SECRET 20: STAY AWAY FROM STIRRING THE HORNETS' NEST

Stay away from stirring the hornets' nest. What do I mean? I have seen many well-meaning people become extremely zealous after their deliverance and go on a mission to go further and dig deeper, looking for "more." They start poking around in their souls instead of simply resting in what God did for them in their deliverance. As they slowly begin to regain control of their lives after years of living in bondage, they then start picking fights with the devil. Well, if you look for a hornet, you just might find a hornets' nest.

> Whoever digs a pit may fall into it; whoever breaks through a wall may be bitten by a snake.
>
> —ECCLESIASTES 10:8, NIV

I love this verse because it exemplifies what we New Yorkers embody—and that's "mind your own business." If heaven has put it on your heart that you need to be delivered in more areas, then rest in that, thanking God for what He's already done. Trust that the Word of God is working and that the Holy Spirit will alert you when it is time to pursue another deliverance. When folks start poking around looking for another demon, the devil will show up to attack them. Then what should have been a time of post-deliverance healing and recovery actually becomes a time of warfare and turmoil. This verse says that a person who breaks open an old wall might fail to realize that a snake had been living there for a long time—and it will fight to stay and will even bite. We shouldn't bother with demons without authorization from heaven; even then, deliverance should always be done not with unregulated zeal but with God-sent authority through a commission.

Sometimes people not only go poking around their own souls looking for demons but also stir up the hornets' nests in other people's lives, causing all kinds of trouble. Some even go to an extreme and attend church services that promote this kind of thinking. Unfortunately many of those who attend such services end up as casualties of the war.

Don't become a casualty of war. *Rest in your freedom,* and don't stir up the hornets' nest.

SECRET 21: STAY AWAY FROM DELIVERANCE IDOLATRY

Wherefore, my dearly beloved, flee from idolatry.

—1 CORINTHIANS 10:14

Idolatry comes in many forms. I'm glad the apostle Paul chose not to be specific in this verse. So, what's an idol? It is anything—*anything*—that takes our attention, devotion, and admiration away from God. In much the same way that heathens worship tangible idols, parents can idolize their children and people can idolize their cars, their careers, and so on.

Idolatry can take many different forms in the church as well. Many idolize ministry, while others idolize the church. And there is also such a thing as *deliverance idolatry*—which takes place when everything in a person's life revolves around deliverance, the deliverance ministry, or the demonic. Here's a news flash: the church doesn't exist for deliverance ministry, and the early apostles didn't turn the world upside down by preaching the ministry of deliverance—they preached the gospel.

Note: *Deliverance is not the gospel*; it's part of the

benefit package of salvation. It is not the main message. The gospel is strictly the death, burial, and resurrection of Jesus Christ.

Please know that deliverance may have been the method God used to help set you free from some inner conflict after your salvation experience, but it should not dominate your every thought; nor should preaching deliverance become your life's mission. When everything becomes a potential deliverance session, you are taking away from the efficacy of Christ's work on the cross and steering into deliverance idolatry. Yes, there is such a thing, and many in the deliverance camp are enslaved to it.

A symptom of deliverance idolatry is when the excitement of deliverance engulfs individuals to the point that they focus more on demons and deliverance than on the person of Christ, on Scripture, or on developing intimacy with the Holy Spirit. Sometimes I wonder whether our idolatry of the ministry of deliverance is causing people to attract demons. Why? Because the following passage tells us that there are demons behind every idol.

> Am I saying that food offered to idols has
> some significance, or that idols are real gods?
> No, not at all. I am saying that these sacri-
> fices are offered to demons, not to God. And
> I don't want you to participate with demons.
> —1 CORINTHIANS 10:19–20, NLT

Now, don't get me wrong. I'm not saying that if a person has deliverance idolatry, he or she automatically has a demon. No. I'm saying that anything that takes the place of Christ in our lives and the Great Commission of preaching the gospel could become idolatry. I am also not saying that we need to stop promoting deliverance; we can enjoy the beautiful ministry of deliverance from demons, but everything must be done in moderation.

SECRET 22: STAY AWAY FROM THE UNCLEAN THING

The Scriptures are very clear that one of the rules of engagement in spiritual warfare is to stay away from anything impure or unclean. You can't stay free from darkness if you're still playing with darkness.

> Wherefore come out from among them, and
> be ye separate, saith the Lord, and touch not
> the unclean thing; and I will receive you.
> —2 CORINTHIANS 6:17

Notice that this text doesn't say "don't touch anything sinful"; instead, it uses the word *unclean*. I go into the differentiations in my second book (*The Secrets to Generational Curses*) quite extensively, but *unclean* and *sin* aren't the same thing. *Sin* refers to transgression against God's law and requires punishment, but *unclean* means ceremonially unfit for the Lord's service. Being ceremonially clean was a requirement for priests who served in the tabernacle or temple, as well as for Nazarites. So, a person who was "unclean" wasn't necessarily in sin but was unfit for service.

There are things you might do that aren't sinful, but heaven doesn't want you participating in them. What are some examples of unclean things that affect your freedom?

- listening to questionable music
- watching questionable movies

- drinking alcohol (even low-percentage alcohol, such as wine)
- getting tattoos

These are just a few of the unclean things that aren't necessarily sinful but prove to be a stumbling block for many and do indeed open the door to committing further sins. Now, I'm not suggesting that you should embrace legalism, but neither is it safe to say these four activities can be considered clean. They fall under the category of "unclean." If you find that God used you frequently after you were set free from demonic involvement in your life but now things have slowed down, well...ask the Holy Spirit to reveal to you what unclean things you have been participating in that are causing the anointing in your life to subside.

Pray this prayer, asking the Holy Spirit to reveal anything that could be considered unclean, and then write those things down.

Holy Spirit, I ask that You reveal to me whether I have been touching the unclean thing and causing Your presence to subside in my life. [Write what the Holy Spirit reveals to you in the space provided.]

_____

_____

_____

_____

Lord, I repent of these things. I renounce them now, and I commit to never touch those things again. I make a covenant with You to live for You with all my heart, soul, and strength from this day forward. In Jesus' name, amen.

SECRET 23: STAY AWAY FROM UNFORGIVENESS

I have held back this last "staying away" secret because an enormous number of books are dedicated to discussing unforgiveness, but the Scriptures are clear: if you don't walk in forgiveness of others, the Lord won't forgive you (Matt. 18:21–35). This is important in the area of deliverance because many people in the church don't believe in this ministry. In their joy many believers who genuinely received deliverance went and told others, hoping they would believe too, but their testimonies were met with fierce skepticism. Nothing kills your joy and newfound freedom like another Christian criticizing it or wanting to argue that a Christian "can't have a demon." Sometimes the lack of compassion from those who are supposed to show it the most can cause a person to become offended, and the fiercer the offense, the deeper the problem of unforgiveness will be.

If there is anything I have asked God to help me with the most, it is my forgiveness walk. Discernment ministries have released countless videos about me. Many of the videos made about my person can honestly be proven wrong, but instead I choose to turn the other cheek. I'm totally okay with being held accountable publicly, especially if I said something wrong publicly, but these people make thumbnail pictures of me with exaggerated features in caricature, including devil horns. Trust me when I tell you that walking in forgiveness has been my greatest challenge to keeping my freedom.

But unforgiveness allows hell to outsmart us and take advantage of our weakness.

> When you forgive this man, I forgive him, too. And when I forgive whatever needs to be forgiven, I do so with Christ's authority for your benefit, so that Satan will not outsmart us. For we are familiar with his evil schemes.
> —2 CORINTHIANS 2:10–11, NLT

This is how powerful unforgiveness can be in placing a Christian back into bondage. Demons can gain reentry by enforcing their evil scheme of unforgiveness, causing a believer to focus on the offense rather than on the cross. Every time a heckling video about me is uploaded on social media, I truly have learned to get on my knees and pray for the content creator.

I remember one time a couple of Christian content creators completed a critique on my first book (*The Secrets to Deliverance*) and rated it as the "second-worst Christian book" they had ever read. I was deeply hurt and offended at that, but instead of attacking, I chose to pray for them both. Later that day my book shot up to number one on the bestseller list, and it has remained a bestseller since 2018. My book was also a catalyst for Greg Locke's movie, *Come Out in Jesus Name*, which reached number four at the box office the day it was released. Forgiveness works!

Note to all discernment ministers: I forgive you, and I will continue to turn the other cheek. I pray that God blesses your ministry. (I sincerely mean that, with my conscience bearing witness before God.)

ONE SIN DOESN'T MAKE YOU DEMONIZED

Let this sink in as we begin to close this chapter: you don't need to be re-delivered anytime you sin. I decided to add this point because I have noticed a dangerous trend of Christians running to make appointments for deliverance sessions when they mess up once, twice, or multiple times in a certain area. *You are not demonized every time you fall into sin or dwell on temptation.*

If it's any consolation, I am tempted and battle with sin quite frequently, just like any other believer. Those in the demon-slayers camp, including my friends Mike Signorelli, Isaiah Saldivar, and Vlad Savchuk, don't have special privileges or powers to resist temptation. No, if anything, we struggle with sin *more* than the average person because of the heavy responsibility associated with being a leading voice of deliverance. So, what do Pagani, Mike, Isaiah, and Vlad do when we mess up and sin? We repent. We confess our sins in prayer, and we depend on the Holy Spirit to help us not do it again. Not once have I considered myself "demonized" when I am going through a season of really struggling against sin. My dependency is on the blood of Jesus, not a deliverance session.

Am I saying that Christian aren't demonized? No. I'm encouraging you to *rest in Jesus*, and when you sin, understand that you simply need forgiveness for your sin, just like anyone else. The Bible tells us what to do when we sin in our Christian walk:

> But if we confess our sins to him, he is faithful and just to forgive us our sins and to cleanse us from all wickedness.
> —1 JOHN 1:9, NLT

Not all of the "staying away" secrets refer to sins per se—although some do. They relate more to having wrong theology, thinking in faulty ways, following the wrong rules, and so on. The kingdom

147

of darkness uses these as traps and stumbling blocks in the believer's walk with Christ. This is why Proverbs 1:17 says, "If a bird sees a trap being set, it knows to *stay away*" (NLT, emphasis added).

Make it your business to stay away from these traps. I know this might sound crazy, but faulty theology—wrong beliefs about how to carry out the Christian faith—can cause all types of disappointments, frustration, and setbacks that God is not obligated to fix. Why? Because those rules and regulations about deliverance have been set up by human philosophy, wrong theological concepts, and unbiblical declarations. This is why Paul says that the best way to avoid any of these traps is to "be dead" to them.

> You have died with Christ, and he has set you free from the spiritual powers of this world. So why do you keep on following the rules of the world?
> —COLOSSIANS 2:20, NLT

A dead person doesn't fall for a trap. It's hard to tempt someone who is dead because there is nothing alive within the person to crave those temptations. Not only that, but a dead person doesn't become enslaved to a set of rules that is neither founded in Scripture nor given freely to us by the efficacy of Christ's work on the cross. The rules of the world only cause enslavement in other areas, and they often lead to an extreme version of deliverance that becomes the poster child for every antagonist, troll, and heckler to use against the ministry of deliverance.

Let's pray.

> *Thank You, Jesus, for using the words of this chapter to equip me in maintaining my deliverance. Help me stay away from all that was mentioned, and empower me to live completely dependent on Scripture and the understanding of my identity in You so I can walk out my freedom. In Jesus' name, amen.*

CHAPTER 5

THE SECRETS OF RECOMMENDED ABIDANCE

I am the vine; you are the branches. Those who *remain in* me, and I in them, will produce much fruit. For apart from me you can do nothing.

—JOHN 15:5, NLT
EMPHASIS ADDED

As ye have therefore received Christ Jesus the Lord, so walk ye in him: Rooted and built up *in him*, and stablished in the faith, as ye have been taught, abounding therein with thanksgiving.

—COLOSSIANS 2:6–7
EMPHASIS ADDED

And they are not *connected to Christ*, the head of the body. For he holds the whole body together with its joints and ligaments, and it grows as God nourishes it.

—COLOSSIANS 2:19, NLT
EMPHASIS ADDED

I KNOW THAT AT this point you may still be wondering why this is not another revelatory book giving insight into deep things of the demonic. In my previous two books, I gave you strategies for how to be set free from the toughest cases of demonic bondage and how to break the strongholds in your bloodline. But here I'm giving you the user manual of the deliverance ministry so your freedom can remain perpetual. So, please excuse me if I spend more time in this book turning on the light than focusing on the darkness.

Jesus said it was important that the church stay connected to Him. Many in the deliverance movement have strayed away from the simplicity of depending on Jesus more than on an exorcism or a deliverance minister. Demons love it when we draw our attention away from the light and put it on the darkness. This is why I'm going to spend almost this entire chapter turning on the light and keeping you there—because the light is the place where God dwells:

> This then is the message which we have heard of him, and declare unto you, that God is light, and in him is no darkness at all....But

> if we walk in the light, as he is in the light,
> we have fellowship one with another, and the
> blood of Jesus Christ his Son cleanseth us
> from all sin.
>
> —1 JOHN 1:5, 7

Staying connected to the light is the same as staying connected to the true vine. Jesus said that we are to remain in Him (John 15:5). We are not to remain in seeking demons, overemphasizing deliverance, or lifting deliverance ministers up on pedestals. No. We must look to Christ alone by faith alone. Jesus—and Jesus only—is our sufficiency. We are the branches, and our source of life is the vine. The vine has the light, and if we remain in Him, we will walk in the light and not dwell in darkness. I have been able to survive this long in deliverance ministry only because I completely depend on Jesus as my sufficiency. Without Him I can do absolutely nothing.

The gospel is enough. The gospel has enough light to push back all the forces of darkness. When you stay connected to the light, you are connected to the gospel of Jesus. I exhort you to place a high value on Scripture because "[His] word is a lamp unto [your] feet, and a light unto [your] path" (Ps. 119:105).

This is what Jesus meant when He said we can't bear fruit without Him. He didn't tell us to remain in reading deliverance books (although there is nothing wrong with reading them). Nor did He say to maintain a good diet of watching deliverance videos (although there is nothing wrong with that either).

Important note: Alexander Pagani is not your source of freedom. The gospel is your source of freedom—that and valuing the wisdom of Scripture. Why? Because it is the truth that will set you free. So place your eyes and your faith on Jesus alone.

Stay connected to Jesus, because it is *in Him* that deliverance takes place—not in Pagani or any other deliverance ministry. I know we don't like to admit this, but there is often an unhealthy dependency on deliverance ministers instead of on Christ. Take a few moments to pray a prayer of repentance if you have placed more value on deliverance ministries than on Jesus.

The most powerful revelation believers can have

against the forces of darkness is knowing who they are connected to. As I indicated in chapter 1, this secret is one of the most detrimental to the kingdom of darkness, because had the devil known whom he was killing, he would not have crucified the Lord of glory (1 Cor. 2:8).

SECRET 24: BE ROOTED, BUILT UP, AND ESTABLISHED IN CHRIST

Understanding this concept is so important: you are more powerful than you could ever realize—not because of your gifts or special abilities but because of the redemptive work Jesus accomplished on the cross. As a result heaven is requiring three things of you: to stay rooted, built up, and established in Christ, as the following verse says:

> As ye have therefore received Christ Jesus the Lord, so walk ye in him: rooted and built up *in him*, and stablished in the faith, as ye have been taught, abounding therein with thanksgiving.
>
> —COLOSSIANS 2:6–7
> EMPHASIS ADDED

What does it mean to *stay rooted*? It means to place your faith so deeply in Jesus and to be so grounded in Scripture that you are unmoved. The parable of the sower says that the seeds that fell on stony ground grew quickly but then soon withered away. Why? Because they had no roots (Matt. 13:5–6). Roots take time to go deep; they are not in a hurry to grow. Roots need to be secure and deep enough to support the growth of the plant.

Once you are rooted, it's time to be *built up*. Notice that the direction is upward, not downward. You build *up* by allowing the wisdom of God to lead your life. The Bible says that "by wisdom a house is built" (Prov. 24:3, NIV). The Scriptures also say that Christ is our wisdom:

> But of him are ye in Christ Jesus, who of God is made unto us wisdom, and righteousness, and sanctification, and redemption.
> —1 CORINTHIANS 1:30

Wisdom will cause you to know how to build your house. Imagine building a house with no wisdom—the builder might construct something, but it won't be a house. Building a house requires specific instructions and requirements to make it what it is meant to be. Heaven will give you wisdom in how to maintain your deliverance, and if you follow it, you will be happy with the result.

Once the house is built, by default it becomes *established*, meaning it's time to move in. No one moves into a house without knowing the house is established and secure enough to hold a family. The same is true with Christ and your freedom.

When individuals aren't established in their freedom, they are free for a couple of days, but then when trials and tribulations arise, they quickly backslide or need more deliverance sessions. When you are *in Christ*, your roots go deep, and you build on that foundation until you finish the house and establish it. Then you dwell in it and enjoy the benefits.

SECRET 25: BE THANKFUL

Being thankful is the glue that upholds these powerful revelations. If a sense of gratitude is not birthed as you learn about being "in Christ," then truly you're not *in Christ*, because the overwhelming response to such privilege given to the believer is gratefulness—being thankful for all He has done.

Nothing grieves the heart of God more than ungrateful people, those who don't cherish what Jesus purchased for us on the cross of Calvary. The Scriptures say that we are to abound in thanksgiving (Col. 2:7). Why? Because thankfulness comes from a place of contentment. We can be content when we know that *in Christ*, we have everything we need to sustain us. This removes our unhealthy dependence on deliverance sessions. (Note that I'm not criticizing deliverance sessions—they make us aware of our completeness in Christ.)

> And ye are complete in him, which is the head of all principality and power.
> —Colossians 2:10

When you understand you're already complete in Jesus, your heart's response is contentment, knowing that your sufficiency rests in Him. Being complete means that you lack nothing. All your mental, emotional, and spiritual needs are met in Christ.

The devil and his demons can't withstand the potency of grateful Christians who verbally and internally express their thankfulness. This is why the Scripture says that Jesus is the "head over all principality and power." Notice the connection between resting in the sufficiency of Jesus and how He helps us deal with the demonic.

SECRET 26: COMMIT TO BEING "IN HIM"

The next concept I want to talk about is simple but necessary. Personally I don't think this topic is discussed enough: the revelation of being "in Him." Numerous scriptures give a doctrinal view of our position in Christ, but I want to discuss it in more practical terms regarding the Christian life. Two things are the result of being in Him, and both regard staying connected—to the Word and to a local church. Disconnection in either of these two areas is the devil's playground, and it is tripping up many believers.

Staying Connected to the Word

If I could write a whole book on this point, I would, because I think the outcry of many Christians about deliverance ministers is that we don't place a high enough value on Scripture. Although that might be true for some in the deliverance ministry, it is not the case with me.

Alexander Pagani has always placed a high value on Scripture. God's Word is God's wisdom. If you want to sustain your freedom, then you must, above all else, highly value Scripture and spend time both reading and studying it. If you don't, you run the risk of your wisdom becoming contaminated—and such wisdom later can become demonic.

> For jealousy and selfishness are not God's kind of wisdom. Such things are earthly, unspiritual, and demonic.
>
> —James 3:15, nlt

You never want to get to the place where you're not daily feasting on the Word. Jesus is the Word. The Bible says that "in the beginning was the Word, and the Word was with God and the Word was God" (John 1:1). But it also says that the Word became flesh, and "the darkness comprehended it not" (v. 5). And Jesus said, "The flesh profits nothing. The words that I speak to you are spirit, and they are life" (John 6:63, nkjv).

When a believer doesn't get into the Word, the flesh starts to profit—this is why it all starts in the Word.

Staying Connected to the Local Church

This next point is just as important as the last one. Not only is Jesus the Word and are His words life-giving spirit, but His church is also His body.

> And they are not connected to Christ, the head of the body. For he holds the whole body together with its joints and ligaments, and it grows as God nourishes it.
> —COLOSSIANS 2:19, NLT

Oh, how I wish the deliverance crowd would value church attendance, but many don't. My wife and I have noticed a dangerous culture emerging within deliverance ministries: Everyone is "in transition." For whatever reason, many feel that if the local church doesn't embrace deliverance, then they shouldn't attend. *No.* The fact that your local church might not embrace deliverance is no excuse to stay home or not be connected to a local assembly. Why? Because the church is the body of Christ. He is the head, and we are the body parts.

The body part can't exist without the body or the head. Neither can the deliverance person exist without connecting to the local church. Let me say this again: If you're not part of a local church, then you're out of order. There is protection from the evil one when we are connected to the local *ekklesia*. When we are submitted to the governing body of elders and leaders, they will care for our souls and hold us accountable.

You can't say you love Jesus and not love His body. The verse above states that Jesus causes the body to grow—not a body part but the whole body. So many aren't walking in their freedom because they are violating this one principle. Stay connected to the church. Being a member of the church is a form of being *in Him*.

Another reason I encourage folks to become connected to a local church is because *everything is not a demon*. Some sicknesses are the result not of an infestation of demons but of the fall of humankind. In such cases professional or medical help might be required, but if not, Scripture commands us to have the elders of the church anoint the sick in the name of the Lord and pray the prayer of faith. Don't be "spooky"; instead, follow biblical protocol.

> Are any of you sick? You should call for the elders of the church to come and pray over you, anointing you with oil in the name of

the Lord. Such a prayer offered in faith will heal the sick, and the Lord will make you well. And if you have committed any sins, you will be forgiven.

—JAMES 5:14–15, NLT

Fall in Love With Jesus

There is no substitute for a believer falling desperately in love with Jesus. When you're in love, you strive to please the person in everything you do. This love is based not on works but on the heart's trust. One reason I can remain pure in every aspect of my life is that I am desperately in love with Jesus. I wholeheartedly trust what He did on the cross as the only means for my salvation and my daily sanctification. I'm not referring to legalism or a works-based sanctification. No. I'm talking about a total dependence on Him and His love to keep me from falling. I choose to remain in the love of God as Jesus commanded us to do. I commit to true biblical love that is dependent on the person of Jesus, not on deliverance, deliverance ministers, or even preoccupation with the demonic. *Fall in love with Jesus.*

> Keep yourselves in the love of God, looking
> for the mercy of our Lord Jesus Christ unto
> eternal life.
>
> —JUDE 21

SECRET 27: WALK IN LOVE

The gasoline that starts the engine of freedom can be summed up in one word: *love*. The Book of Galatians tells us that "faith...worketh by love" (5:6); without love, the car won't start, and your journey of freedom won't even begin. This revelation of love is the missing link.

The ministry of deliverance is a ministry of love. Charity is at the root of all we are and do. As a matter of fact the essence of our inheritance is the fact that God loves us and has given us the spirit of love.

Note: Demons cannot handle love. It suffocates them.

> That Christ may dwell in your hearts by
> faith; that ye, being rooted and grounded
> in love, may be able to comprehend with all
> saints what is the breadth, and length, and
> depth, and height; and to know the love of

Christ, which passeth knowledge, that ye
might be filled with all the fulness of God.

—EPHESIANS 3:17–19

This is why, in Ephesians 3, the primary focus of
the apostle Paul's prayer for the church in Ephesus
was that God would reveal to them the inheritance
of love and an understanding of it.

Knowing that you're loved—and how vast is
God's love for you—will keep you from opening
any doors of your soul when demons bang on them
with rejection and abandonment. Notice how the
passage indicates that understanding this inheritance of love causes you to be filled with God.
There is no room for the demonic if you're filled
with love.

SECRET 28: GOVERN YOUR ATTITUDE (THE BE-ATTITUDES)

What is an attitude? It is "a settled way of thinking
or feeling about someone or something" or "a position of the body proper to or implying an action or
mental state."[1]

Having the right mental state is so very important because a bad attitude can stunt your growth.

165

A famous saying is that "your attitude, not your aptitude, will determine your altitude." This is so true, even for the kingdom. Even in the darkest of scenarios, having the right attitude will boost your strength, especially if you know that the task at hand will be rough. Demons love to sap your strength by killing your attitude. This is why the apostle Paul encourages us to take on the attitude of Jesus:

> You must have the same attitude that Christ Jesus had.
> —PHILIPPIANS 2:5, NLT

Christ endured so much to become our atoning sacrifice. The Bible gives a breakdown of just how much He went through to take on the penalty for our sins. No other human being would have been able to endure it. In the Book of Romans, Paul wrote that even when we were yet sinners, Jesus died for us (5:8). But in the middle of all that, as sinners turned against Him and crucified Him, the Book of Hebrews says "the joy" of what was coming caused Jesus' attitude to remain focused—even when He was on the cross and cried out, "My God, My God, why have You forsaken Me?" The

Gospel accounts paint a grim picture, but look at what the Book of Hebrews says. This verse tells us what happens when our attitudes remain positive:

> Looking unto Jesus the author and finisher of our faith; who for the joy that was set before him endured the cross, despising the shame, and is set down at the right hand of the throne of God.
>
> —HEBREWS 12:2

I don't know many people who would consider the cross to be *joyful*, but Jesus did. This is why Paul tells us to have the same attitude that Jesus had—the same mental state He had while on the earth. This is possible only if there is an attitude shift. Now you know why, in the Sermon on the Mount, the first topic Jesus covered was our attitudes.

Your deliverance will be maintained when you get an attitude adjustment. Demons hate joyful Christians and can't stand to be around them. This is why the Gospels, the Book of Acts, and the Epistles spend an enormous amount of time discussing being joyful during trials and tribulations. It's all about attitude.

Blessed are the *poor in spirit*: for theirs is the kingdom of heaven. Blessed are they that *mourn*: for they shall be comforted. Blessed are the *meek*: for they shall inherit the earth. Blessed are they which do *hunger and thirst* after righteousness: for they shall be filled. Blessed are the *merciful*: for they shall obtain mercy. Blessed are the *pure in heart*: for they shall see God. Blessed are the *peacemakers*: for they shall be called the children of God. Blessed are they which are *persecuted* for righteousness' sake: for theirs is the kingdom of heaven. Blessed are ye, when men shall revile you, and persecute you, and shall say all manner of evil against you falsely, for my sake.

—MATTHEW 5:3–11
EMPHASIS ADDED

The Attitude of Being Poor in Spirit

If there is anything this generation is obviously struggling with, it is the "pride of life" (1 John 2:16)—overemphasizing that "we are OK" and "we know what to do." This is precisely what is wrong with this generation. Jesus rebuked the Laodicean church for not being poor of spirit:

> You say, "I am rich, have become wealthy, and have need of nothing"—and do not know that you are wretched, miserable, poor, blind, and naked.
>
> —REVELATION 3:17, NKJV

There is a secret to remaining poor in spirit: it is not about money but about attitude. Being poor in spirit means that you *always* need God. I know this might sound old-fashioned, but what has kept me serving God for the last thirty years of my life has been my utter need of Him. I'm never in the place where I'm self-sufficient.

Note: We need Christ, and the gospel, more and more.

As long as I have breath in my lungs, I'm always in the place of "pray[ing] without ceasing" (1 Thess. 5:17); it takes me only a quick second to say a prayer—"Lord, help me"—and declare my need of Him even in the simplest of tasks. Being poor in spirit causes you to know that you need Him. You are always a child and a citizen of His kingdom.

Maintaining an attitude of being poor in spirit means you depend on your rights in the kingdom and the blessing that comes with being a citizen of heaven. In the natural infants are always poor in the sense that they own nothing and do not worry about anything; they totally depend on their parents. Ideally, citizens have no worries regarding their welfare either, because they know they have rights. This is worth shouting. As both a child of God and a citizen of His kingdom, all you must do to activate the privileges and blessings is to become poor and dependent—this truly activates the kingdom.

> But seek first the kingdom of God and His righteousness, and all these things shall be added to you.
>
> —MATTHEW 6:33, NKJV

The Attitude of Mourning

Having an attitude of mourning doesn't mean that we walk around feeling sad all day or that we live in a culture and environment of grief. *No.* It means that we always have a readiness to mourn over the things God mourns over, including sin, worldliness, and so on. Mourning keeps us from becoming *de*sensitized to anything that might open the door to the devil. Sometimes in our immaturity, we give place to the devil by allowing in things that aren't necessarily sinful but are not beneficial to our Christian growth and freedom; they contaminate our ear and eye gates. Mourning will cause us to remain *sensitive* to whatever doesn't please God.

It will also generate a continual cleansing in our lives, as we will perpetually repent and seek heaven to cleanse us from the filth that surrounds us. Look at what the Bible says:

> Sorrow is better than laughter, for by a sad countenance the heart is made better. The heart of the wise is in the house of mourning, but the heart of fools is in the house of mirth.
> —ECCLESIASTES 7:3–4, NKJV

The text says that the wise live in the house of mourning. Oh my—I love that. I never want to get to place where I need cleansing but don't sense that need. I never want to get to a place where I don't feel the conviction of sin in my life and desire cleansing or the need for deliverance, simply carrying on like normal. The verse says that mourning is good for my heart. (Many are dealing with physical heart attacks because they haven't mourned for the sins and the contamination that plague their souls.)

Too many preachers and high-profile ministers lost their mourning a long time ago; because of this, they're not experiencing the comfort of the Holy Spirit as heaven exposes them. Mourners receive comfort because they become aware of their need for repentance and cleansing, and heaven comforts them in that process.

Always stay in the place of mourning. Never lose your mourning over sin, as it will purge you and keep you walking in freedom.

The Attitude of Meekness

Meekness is regulated power. It's not the same as humility (although many think it is). Rather, meekness is having the power to do something but choosing not to. This is why turning the other cheek is truly a display of meekness. Meekness is a fruit of the Spirit, which means it's an impartation the Holy Spirit can give. The Spirit of God grants meekness to those who have just been through deliverance to help regulate and keep them from deliverance idolatry. After receiving deliverance, many become overly excited about their newfound freedom, and they venture off, confronting all kinds of principalities over cities and regions.

They take on a self-imposed assignment of trying to convert every church that doesn't embrace the idea of deliverance. In the end they can develop an arrogance that is noticeable and turns people off.

Note: We are called not to convert the world to the ministry of deliverance but *to preach the death, burial, and resurrection of Jesus.*

Having an attitude of meekness ensures we regulate the authority God has given us without crossing His boundaries. God is not obligated to protect what He never sanctioned. We find an example of this in Scripture, when the children of Israel were told *not* to try to go into the Promised Land outside of God's timing, but in their zeal and defiance they went ahead—and were defeated.

> Moses said, "Why are you now disobeying the LORD's orders to return to the wilderness? It won't work. Do not go up into the land now. You will only be crushed by your enemies because the LORD is not with you."...But the people defiantly pushed ahead toward the hill country, even though neither Moses nor the Ark of the LORD's Covenant left the camp. Then the Amalekites and the Canaanites who lived in those hills came

> down and attacked them and chased them
> back.
>   —NUMBERS 14:41–42, 44–45, NLT

This is what happens when you're not meek. You stir up the hornets' nest and begin to slander demonic dignitaries. You take on a superhero role, and when all hell breaks loose, you run in defeat. The reason Jesus' earthly ministry was so successful and He was able to finish His assignment was that He remained in meekness. The reward for meekness is *inheritance*, which refers to assets bequeathed by a loved one who has passed away. Since "the earth" is the inheritance for those walking in meekness, that means all resources needed to fulfill God's assignment will be supplied to them.

> Take my yoke upon you, and learn of me; for
> I am meek and lowly in heart: and ye shall
> find rest unto your souls.
>   —MATTHEW 11:29

To model the life of Jesus, we need to have the same attitude He had. Stay humble, and stay meek.

The Attitude of Being Hungry and Thirsty

The attitude of being in a continual state of hunger and thirst for the things of God is easy to lose if we don't spend time in the Word. It's easy to be distracted by the cares of this life that choke out the Word so that it doesn't bear fruit. Why is hunger and thirst so important? Because being lukewarm is the Christian's worst enemy. Jesus clearly condemned the sin of being lukewarm:

> But since you are like lukewarm water, neither hot nor cold, I will spit you out of my mouth!
>
> —REVELATION 3:16, NLT

This judgment is severe for those who don't break free from apathy. Unfortunately it's easy to become apathetic to the things of God. Life, family, work, ministry, and many other things can become so burdensome that they drain all the life out of you, and then all you want to do is go to bed. The Son of God paid a heavy price in living on the earth for about thirty-three years to become the atoning sacrifice for our sins—the least we can do is love Him with all our strength.

Have you ever been around a person who had no

zeal, desire, or passion, when you're ready to go all-out for God? It's so annoying. It's burdensome to be around those who do not have the same hunger. I'm sure the Holy Spirit is deeply grieved when the church shows no passion to seek Him. If you want to open wide the door to the demonic, simply allow yourself to become slothful. If any scripture verses depict a person who has reopened the door to the demonic, the following passage does:

> I walked by the field of a lazy person, the vineyard of one with no common sense. I saw that it was overgrown with nettles. It was covered with weeds, and its walls were broken down. Then, as I looked and thought about it, I learned this lesson: A little extra sleep, a little more slumber, a little folding of the hands to rest—then poverty will pounce on you like a bandit; scarcity will attack you like an armed robber.
> —PROVERBS 24:30–34, NLT

If there is one thing Alexander Pagani will never lose, it is my immense hunger for God. Everyone who knows me knows I go hard for God. Why? Because the reward is great—soul satisfaction. I never have a lack in my soul because the promise is clear that I will be filled if I hunger for God. Too many believers who go through deliverance feel unsatisfied afterward because soon after the session, laziness creeps in, and they lose the hunger that led them to get set free. Their thirst for God is quenched by other things, and years (or even months) later, they are living in a perpetual state of dissatisfaction.

Note: When you are filled with more of God, there is no room for demons, curses, or the world.

Who should be the model of our hunger for God? Jesus. If anyone ever showed a relentless pursuit of God and fulfilling of His will, it was the Son of God.

Pray this prayer now, and ask the Holy Spirit to give you a hunger and thirst for righteousness like that of Jesus:

> *Heavenly Father, forgive me for losing my hunger and thirst for You and filling it with other things. Jesus, I know You hate it when Your people are lukewarm, so I repent. Holy Spirit, I humbly ask You*

to make me hungry and thirsty for the
things of God. In Jesus' name, amen.

The Attitude of Mercy

Maybe I should have placed the attitude of mercy at the top of this list. Why? Because currently, especially on social media, mercy is the attribute of God least displayed in our world. We live in a merciless environment (including in many churches), yet mercy is needed to maintain our deliverance. In the Beatitudes as well as in Jesus' other teachings on mercy, the principle is the same: you receive mercy in the same manner and level that you show mercy. This is the only Beatitude whose blessing is conditional upon its execution.

If you want people to show you mercy as you learn to maintain your deliverance, then you must show that same level of mercy to others. This causes you to be more understanding as you walk out your freedom, as no one quickly learns to upgrade his or her defenses against the enemy. Unfortunately many deliverance ministries do not have a follow-up system for the people they help get free, nor do I hear a lot of messages on what happens *after* deliverance. This is why an attitude of mercy is so important.

Note: You're going to mess up as you learn to stay free, and mercy is the method God uses to make sure you don't give up.

The Attitude of Purity of Heart

The attitude of a pure heart is one I personally live by. The reason I can operate so effectively in deliverance ministry is not that I'm special but that I can "see God" clearly during times when I am conducting deliverance—and that is because I have kept my heart pure.

What does it mean to be "pure in heart"? It doesn't necessarily mean to be pure of sin—but it *does* mean to be pure in our motives and perceptions. When those are pure, we can see things clearly, and then God can really show us what needs to get done. The Bible says this:

> To the pure all things are pure, but to those who are defiled and unbelieving nothing is pure; but even their mind and conscience are defiled.
>
> —TITUS 1:15, NKJV

This is why you must not only actively allow the Holy Spirit to purify your heart and mind through deliverance and the ministry of the Word but also ask Him to cleanse your motives and your perceptions.

When I allowed God to help me stop my stinking thinking—especially my default New York City negative attitude—it was like the lens in my spirit shifted into focus. I began to see what God was doing and pattern my actions to be synchronized with His.

Jesus said something in John 5 that reveals how to move in matters of clarity:

> Then Jesus answered and said to them, "Most assuredly, I say to you, the Son can do nothing of Himself, but what He sees the Father do; for whatever He does, the Son also does in like manner."
>
> —JOHN 5:19, NKJV

Notice how this verse says the Son did exactly what He saw the Father doing. That's because Jesus was pure of heart. When you're pure in your motives, intentions, and perceptions, the Father will reveal what He is doing and show you clearly how to do it. The purer you are in your heart, the more God can show you things that normally would be hidden.

> Abstain from all appearance of evil.
> —1 THESSALONIANS 5:22

When you are pure in heart, you're able to discern things that aren't pure, and you can stay away from even the appearance of evil. Oh, how I wish the saints who love Jesus would learn to stay away from anything that might grieve the Holy Spirit.

Note: Purity of heart allows you to stay away from anything you think might grieve the Holy Spirit—even if the Bible is silent on the matter.

The Attitude of the Peacemaker

The attitude of peace is a rarity these days. But peace is also a fruit of the Spirit—an impartation the Spirit gives us. Why? Because peace in this world cannot be achieved apart from Christ. He is the Prince of Peace, even when the world is filled with turmoil. This is why maintaining a peaceful attitude will require effort. The Bible doesn't say "blessed are the peace receivers"; it says "blessed are the peacemakers." Nothing in this world offers peace, so there is nowhere outside Jesus Christ to obtain it. Human civilization has been at war since the early days, back when Cain murdered Abel.

Peace must be fought for and forcefully maintained. The devil operates in the realm of chaos, so it is imperative that you adopt an attitude of peace after you receive your freedom through deliverance. Why? Because I promise you, all hell is going to break loose after your deliverance session.

A sudden chain of events takes place right after your deliverance—designed by Satan to rob you of your peace and cause you to act like a child of disobedience (Eph. 2:2). This is why Jesus said, "Peace I leave with you" (John 14:27). We also find Jesus speaking peace over His disciples many times in the Gospels—using phrases like "Peace, be still!" and "Go in peace." Peace is a fruit of the Holy Spirit because heaven wants to empower you to actively make peace, not wait for peace to happen to you.

This has been a unique year for me, in that I've been making some level of peace with those who have rejected my ministry of deliverance. I have had some phone conversations with those who have opposed my ministry, and to my surprise many of them have also wanted peace. We don't have to agree, but there can be peace between us. If you're a person of influence who is at odds with another person of influence—or anyone, for that matter—allow the Holy Spirit to help you make peace with that person.

Making peace in this way proves to the world that you are a child of God because our God is a God of peace, and through Jesus' atoning sacrifice, we become children of peace. Children receive the benefits of their father, and we must receive all our heavenly Father has to offer. This is why those who make the choice to walk in peace will benefit greatly.

The Attitude of the Persecuted

No one likes to be persecuted. In fact the present-day version of Christianity has taught us to be runners. Too many programs on Christian television and teachings from social media ministries promote escapism. We are always running from confrontation and looking for the easy way out. We are always looking for a day when the demons will take a break and just leave us alone.

Note: Until Jesus returns, demons will never take a "day off" from attacking you, and the world will never stop tempting you. But you will be victorious.

Why is this attitude of the persecuted so important? Because the vast majority of Christians don't believe in the ministry of deliverance, and they will persecute you with words of discouragement, such as "There is no such thing as deliverance" or "You're a heretic for believing a Christian can go through deliverance" or "Christians can't have demons inside them." You must understand that you will be persecuted for your newfound freedom, just like the governments of some countries "revile" and harass the United States because of our Constitution. America invests tons of financial resources in the military because we know that our freedoms could very well be attacked by those who hate democracy. The reason we can live freely in the United States is that we are zealous in defending those freedoms.

Defend your spiritual freedom just as diligently,

while understanding that persecution is part of the package. Jesus said that we will benefit from the kingdom if we accept that we will be persecuted and fight to defend spiritual freedoms.

I'm not talking about having a persecution complex—the feeling or false perception that everyone is against us because we believe in deliverance. Not at all. That's often a sign of rejection issues. Individuals with a persecution complex are annoying, because they always feel hurt that their peers don't agree with them.

Let me say this with all humility: Alexander Pagani is one of the most persecuted voices concerning deliverance in this present time. But not once have I embraced a persecution complex, nor have I ever complained about the hostility targeted at me. And not once have I made a response video to those who heckle me or create videos against me. I'm free from all that. Why? Because the kingdom of God is at my disposal as a child of God, and I have accepted the fact that I will be persecuted because I'm free.

CHAPTER 6

THE SECRETS OF IDENTITY ILLUSTRATIONS

Because of the weakness of your human nature, I am using the illustration [*analogy*] of slavery to help you understand all this.

—ROMANS 6:19, NLT
EMPHASIS ADDED

What *soldier* has to pay his own expenses? What *farmer* plants a vineyard and doesn't have the right to eat some of its fruit? What *shepherd* cares for a flock of sheep and isn't allowed to drink some of the milk? Am I expressing merely a human opinion, or does the law say the same thing?

—1 CORINTHIANS 9:7–8, NLT
EMPHASIS ADDED

Don't you realize that in a race everyone runs, but only one person gets the prize? So run to win! All *athletes* are disciplined in their training. They do it to win a prize that will fade away, but we do it for an eternal prize. So I run with purpose in every step. I am not just shadowboxing. I discipline my body like an athlete, training it to do what it should. Otherwise, I fear that after preaching to others I myself might be disqualified.

—1 Corinthians 9:24–27, nlt
emphasis added

For I am jealous for you with the jealousy of God himself. I promised you as a pure *bride* to one husband—Christ.

—2 Corinthians 11:2, nlt
emphasis added

W E'VE FINALLY REACHED the last chapter of this book, and I am hoping and praying that I have given you enough biblical references for you to walk in victory after your deliverance sessions have ended. We have pointed out the extremities of the deliverance ministry that need to be rejected, as well as truths that need to be embraced. You would do well to go back and read the previous chapters again, slowly digesting them.

Note: The goal of deliverance ministry is that you never come back—the same goal as in any postoperation doctor visit. If you follow the prescribed steps to remain healthy and faithfully take your medication, you will not need to return to the hospital for further surgery, except in extreme cases.

The need for continual deliverance ministry speaks volumes about either the ineffectiveness of the deliverance ministry itself or the unwillingness of those seeking freedom to do what it takes to stay free.

However, I know that if you have made it this far in this book—what I call a user guide—the result will be "absolute holiness" (Ezek. 43:12, NLT), which has always been God's goal for His people. He calls us a "holy nation" (1 Pet. 2:9), so this level of holiness *is* attainable.

The gospel is sufficient. Jesus is sufficient. The Word of God is sufficient. And submitting to God and resisting the devil, as His Word tells us to do, work.

Before we conclude this book, I want to look at several identity comparisons. By this I mean analogies that compare believers to job descriptions or statuses to help them understand ways that God wants us to operate. Although I don't have the space to be exhaustive, I do feel that ending on this topic will help fully persuade you that maintaining your deliverance must become your top priority.

Identity comparisons are found in multiple places in the New Testament epistles and the Synoptic Gospels, in the form of parables or analogies. Examples of this are when Jesus compared us to vineyard workers (Matt. 20:1–16) and to wedding guests (Matt. 22:1–14). In the Romans passage that opened this chapter, the apostle Paul said he was using an analogy to help the church understand a spiritual responsibility (6:19). In other words these analogies give us greater understanding of our identity and responsibility in Christ.

Although many analogies can help us with this, I'm going to focus only on five to close out this book. I think these five analogies are great in helping the saints understand their Christian responsibilities:

1. The soldier

2. The athlete

3. The shepherd

4. The farmer

5. The wife (the bride)

Let's begin.

SECRET 29: BE A LOYAL SOLDIER

Let's start with the most obvious analogy of all, one that appears the most in the New Testament and may be the best-known among believers—that of a soldier. Believers are compared to soldiers in the Book of Ephesians, which goes into detail to describe our armor and our mental state in preparing for war. (Read Ephesians 6:10–18.)

What makes someone a loyal soldier? Let's first consider what a soldier is primarily known for and why the role of the soldier exists. Being a soldier has three key aspects. Let's look at them closely.

Training

Soldiers are trained to do battle, to never lose a fight, and to know everything about their enemy. What does this mean for believers? Well, we need to take on a "boot camp" mentality. God will allow us to encounter different trials and tests to fortify us and train us in the battle. I love what the author of Hebrews said with regard to training, and I think he wrote this with the soldier analogy in mind:

> Solid food is for those who are mature, who
> *through training* have the skill to recognize
> the difference between right and wrong.
> —HEBREWS 5:14, NLT
> EMPHASIS ADDED

I love this verse because it promotes the idea that believers need to break away from laziness and codependency on any deliverance minister by rolling up their sleeves and starting their own training.

How do you train for spiritual battle? Discipline yourself through daily reading your Bible and daily spending time in worship and prayer. Faithfully attend church as often as you can. You have begun the rigorous process of training how to fight. And once you have learned how to fight, you are ready for combat.

Combat

When the Lord determines that believers are ready, He places them into small battles or combat. If you want to maintain your freedom, you're going to have to fight for it. You fight by taking control of your mind and casting down imaginations, learning to discipline the way you speak, and getting involved in different outreaches in your church. All these things involve combat. Standing up for truth in a lukewarm, evil society can also be a form of combat. In the US Army "every soldier is trained and prepared for possible deployment" and "any soldier can be deployed."[1] Even those assigned to less-obvious levels of warfare are called to action during times of need.

I hope you fight like a warrior until the end. I have given you three books of deep-level training in the demonic and spiritual warfare. Don't allow them to be just head knowledge for you. Take up the weapon of the Word of God and fight.

Endurance

The more you fight, the more you will be able to handle in a fight. The Book of James says that trials and tribulation work *endurance* in us.

> Dear brothers and sisters, when troubles of any kind come your way, consider it an opportunity for great joy. For you know that when your faith is tested, your endurance has a chance to grow. So let it grow, for when your endurance is fully developed, you will be perfect and complete, needing nothing.

—JAMES 1:2–4, NLT

Endurance is the ability to withstand long periods of fighting or to tolerate multiple attacks on your person. Soldiers are typically known for one thing: *not quitting*. They are trained to fight to the death, and they will endure just about anything that comes without flinching, because the goal of winning the battle is more important than anything else.

The apostle Paul urged us to become that kind of soldier. He wanted us to be able to endure hardship. Far too many saints are weak and give up too easily. I want you to fight to maintain the freedom of your last deliverance session and request another one *only* if you are left with no other option. No matter how much it hurts—no matter how hard the devil is attacking you because of your deliverance—endure, and fight back.

> Thou therefore endure hardness, as a good soldier of Jesus Christ. No man that warreth entangleth himself with the affairs of this life; that he may please him who hath chosen him to be a soldier.
>
> —2 TIMOTHY 2:3–4

You're not just a saint; you're a soldier in the army of the Lord, and you are required to take up arms and fight. If not, you will receive a dishonorable discharge.

Don't allow yourself to get caught up with the cares of this life. Learn everything you need to know about the ministry of deliverance and the demonic, and fight back. You have been mandated to fight. You are required to fight. God chose *you* to fight. Now fight, soldier.

SECRET 30: LIVE LIKE A DISCIPLINED ATHLETE

The comparison of the believer to an athlete is found all throughout Paul's writings. I think it speaks to us very clearly regarding discipline. So, not only are we soldiers, fighting God's battles, but we are also athletes. Paul wrote about this analogy numerous times because at that time, the Greek and Roman cultures were known for their competitive games. The Greeks Paul was writing to would have been familiar with the footraces run in the Isthmian Games at Corinth every two years.[2]

Athletes are known for three things, and I want to take a few moments to look at them more closely.

Competing

I believe Paul used the analogy of an athlete for one reason: competition. I know that being competitive has a negative connotation to many Christians, but truly it doesn't always have to be a self-centered exercise. Every successful athlete must have a competitive edge or won't make the team. Likewise, something inside you must scream, "I'm not going to let the devil win." Anyone who joins a team should have that "we're going to win" spirit.

Christ chose for you to win. Don't allow religion to convince you that being competitive is a sin. It's not—being ambitious is sinful, but heaven wants you to have an athletic mindset and understand the culture of an athlete. Why? Because when you join a team, you no longer represent yourself but the team that chose you.

Representing

I truly think that when Christians fail to fight back, they misrepresent the kingdom. You've been selected to be part of the greatest team on earth. But failure to maintain your freedom makes your team look bad. (I'm not saying multiple deliverance sessions are bad, but *why* are you having to go back for continual deliverance?) When you stand your ground like a true athlete, you represent your team well.

Winning

Winning must be the goal of all athletes. But victory can be achieved only through two things: discipline and rules. Look at the following scripture:

> Don't you realize that in a race everyone runs, but only one person gets the prize? So run to win! *All athletes are disciplined* in their training. They do it to win a prize that will fade away, but we do it for an eternal prize. So I run with purpose in every step. I am not just shadowboxing. I discipline my body like an athlete, training it to do what it should. Otherwise, I fear that after preaching to others I might be disqualified.
> —1 CORINTHIANS 9:24–27, NLT
> EMPHASIS ADDED

As you can see, discipline is the greatest friend of the athlete. Without it, winning will not be possible. Discipline includes the ritual of doing something over and over again until it's perfected.

Maintaining your freedom involves the discipline of your mind. Discipline it repeatedly until you get to the point of needing a deliverance only in extreme cases.

The second way athletes win the prize is by following the rules. Look at this verse:

> Athletes cannot win the prize unless they follow the rules.
> —2 TIMOTHY 2:5, NLT

You can't violate God's rules of freedom and expect to remain free. If you play with sin, you will open the door for demons to return. You can't expect to stay free if you break the rules of keeping the door closed. It's foolish for athletes to expect to win a prize if they have been violating the rules of the competition.

Staying Delivered Is a Marathon

Most of you who are reading this last chapter will have read all the previous chapters. You didn't sprint your way here; rather, you took your time pondering each secret because you didn't want to rush past anything that might be important to maintaining your freedom. Deliverance is not a sprint; it is a marathon. There is no need to rush anything. Take your time, learn each concept written in this book, and you will see that by the time you master them, you will already be reaching the finish line. Don't burn out. Run with patience the race set before you (Heb. 12:1).

> I...saw under the sun, that the race is not to the swift, nor the battle to the strong, neither yet bread to the wise, nor yet riches to men of understanding, nor yet favour to men of skill; but time and chance happeneth to them all.
>
> —ECCLESIASTES 9:11

SECRET 31: SHEPHERD YOUR SOUL

I know you may not be used to hearing this, but you are truly the one responsible to watch over your own soul; it's not up to your local pastor. Yes, pastors play an important role in guarding our souls, but they are not with us 24/7, and we shouldn't place that kind of burden on them. Ultimately each of us must shepherd our own soul.

It's your personal responsibility to learn how your pastor shepherds your soul and then replicate that when the pastor isn't around. As shepherds, pastors do three things.

Feed

The main goal of any pastor is to feed God's people. Pastors spend countless hours in the Word preparing sermons to help their congregations grow in their Christian faith. To shepherd your soul, then, you must practice your own personal Bible studies and spend time digging in to the Scriptures. Feed yourself.

Guide

Pastors guide their sheep to green pastures and still waters. It's their responsibility to make sure the sheep are led to safe places and not endangered. The same must be said about your soul. The Holy Spirit will indicate when you need to remove yourself from places that could open the doors to the demonic or lead to temptation. But He will not do the removing for you; it's something you must do as the true pastor of your own soul.

Protect

The following verse gives the perfect contrast of the true heart of a pastor. Pastors protect the sheep from wolves.

> But he that is an hireling, and not the shepherd, whose own the sheep are not, seeth the wolf coming, and leaveth the sheep, and fleeth: and the wolf catcheth them, and scattereth the sheep.
>
> —JOHN 10:12

You must be ready to give your life in protecting your soul from the devil and the kingdom of darkness. Don't run away when you see the devil trying to creep in; rather, confront him head-on. This means your discernment must be on high alert to *see the wolf coming.* That requires a watchdog style of protection. I'm very militant when it comes to protecting myself. Sometimes it may seem like too much, but too much is never enough. I refuse to allow the wolf to gain an inch in my heart—and so must you.

SECRET 32: CULTIVATE LIKE AN INDUSTRIOUS FARMER

Farming-related comparisons show up many times in the New Testament, and Jesus used them quite frequently in His parables. Paul also related the believer to a farmer. I think this was the most widely recognized analogy by those living in ancient times.

A farmer is different from a shepherd or a soldier. This is the vocation of agriculture, so a different set of rules applies. It requires a lifestyle of patience. Most of us who grew up in the city have no idea what it means to farm, but we do know that farmers who raise crops do at least three things.

Planting

A crop farmer's entire lifestyle and vocation depend on one thing: planting. Everything hinges on sowing seed. If this one thing is not done, even if the land gets the right amount of rain and sunlight, the farmer will go bankrupt.

You must be like a farmer and plant into your own life, whatever that may look like. Reading good Christian books; watching good, wholesome movies; listening to good, clean music; enjoying a walk; spending time with family—all of these, not just the overtly spiritual things, plant good seed in your soul. The idea of planting has to do with *investment*. You must invest in your soul and see yourself like a farmer. Don't be afraid to plant seeds of freedom.

Cultivating

Once farmers plant, then they begin the process of cultivating those seeds by protecting them. The farmers water their seeds and build fences or create barriers around them to protect them from animals and pests. Farmers prune mature plants.

The same is true for you. When you get set free, you don't just walk away, trusting God to keep you that way. No. You must cultivate the ground and treat yourself—your heart and mind—like a field. Without good cultivation there will be no harvest.

Harvesting

The goal of every farmer is the harvest. The harvest means farmers will benefit from all the time and effort they spent planting, cultivating, and watering.

It's not wrong to express joy at your newfound freedom. Tell the whole world about how Jesus set you free—like the man with the legion of demons did in Mark 5:20. Farmers don't hide their harvests. So, don't hide your deliverance. Those who hide their deliverance are bound to lose it.

SECRET 33: BE THE PURE, VIRTUOUS BRIDE OF CHRIST

This last analogy is another that the apostles and Jesus frequently used—that of a bride. All through the Gospels, we find many parables and metaphors related to the idea of a bride or a bridegroom. The apostle Paul had this concept in mind when he oversaw the churches he'd founded. The idea is that the church is the bride of Christ.

> For I am jealous for you with the jealousy of God himself. I promised you as a pure bride to one husband—Christ.
> —2 CORINTHIANS 11:2, NLT

Paul's goal was to keep the church pure while it waited for the Bridegroom to return and take His bride back to His home. In Jesus' parable of the ten virgins (Matt. 25:1–13), it is clear that the women were waiting for the groom's return and that they needed to have oil in their lamps so they could go meet the bridegroom and be welcomed in to the marriage feast.

Why is understanding this bride and bridegroom concept important? It has to do with the seriousness of the vows you take when you get married. Once you take the marriage vows, you are held to the standard of marriage—the highest standard of rules in a relationship.

A bride is held to a higher standard, which can be summed up in the following ways.

Partnership

A bride is a partner to her husband. I have had the privilege of being married to Ibelize Pagani (aka Momma Pagani) for twenty-four years, but we couldn't have gotten this far unless she had partnered with me.

Your freedom can be enforced only if you partner with the Holy Spirit. He won't force you to do so. But choosing to partner with Him means you will submit whenever the Holy Spirit instructs you about something that will help you keep the door shut to the demonic. Partnering requires a contractual agreement. When you went through the ministry of deliverance, you in essence signed a contract of liberty with God. It requires you to partner with Him to continue to guard your soul.

Help

Eve was created to be Adam's "help meet" (Gen. 2:18). In other words Eve was created to *help* Adam meet the requirements God had given him.

You must be a willing helper to your own soul regarding your own freedom. If you won't help yourself, then you won't be able to fulfill all that God requires from you. A wife must help her husband, not stand in his way by being difficult.

Service

Just as a wife serves her husband in various ways, so should the bride of Christ serve Him. We must be willing to serve Him with singleness of heart and mind.

I know this might sound strange, but you must serve your own soul as well. Be willing to listen to your spirit when it's talking to you through discernment. Many believers and ministers are so busy serving and helping others get set free that they have no time to separate from their work and nourish—serve—their own souls. Don't help the world and lose your own soul in the process. Make it your business to focus on your soul, like a bride makes time for her groom.

These are only a few of the identity comparisons found in the Bible. There are many more, but these are some of the most popular—and the most relevant to maintaining your deliverance in the long term.

We've reached the end of this book. I truly believe this was the direction the Holy Spirit wanted to take in helping thousands of believers who have experienced deliverance to maintain it. Freedom will work if you properly use the user guide that God has provided as outlined in Scripture.

Deliverance works. Remaining free is possible. He whom the Son sets free is free indeed. How? If you continue in His Word, you will know the truth, and the truth will make you free.

If you haven't already, I encourage you to read *The Secrets to Deliverance* and *The Secrets to Generational Curses* as complementary teachings to help this book make more sense.

NOTES

CHAPTER 1

1. Timan Wainaina, "What Is a User Guide? Everything You Need to Know (+ Examples)," Scribe, updated September 19, 2023, https://scribehow.com/library/user-guide.
2. Precept Austin, s.v. "secret (*sod*)," updated May 28, 2021, https://www.preceptaustin.org/hebrew_definitions_2.
3. *Merriam-Webster*, s.v. "secret," accessed May 26, 2024, https://www.merriam-webster.com/dictionary/secret.
4. Bible Hub, s.v. "John 14:16," accessed May 29, 2024, https://biblehub.com/john/14-16.htm.
5. Blue Letter Bible, s.v. *"ophthalmos,"* accessed May 29, 2024, https://www.blueletterbible.org/lexicon/g3788/nkjv/tr/0-1/.

CHAPTER 2

1. *Merriam-Webster Thesaurus*, s.v. "absolute," https://www.merriam-webster.com/thesaurus/absolute#thesaurus-entry-1-5.
2. Blue Letter Bible, s.v. *"nagad,"* accessed May 30, 2024, https://www.blueletterbible.org/lexicon/h5046/esv/wlc/0-1/.
3. *Merriam-Webster*, s.v. "specification," accessed May 30, 2024, https://www.merriam-webster.com/dictionary/specification.
4. Blue Letter Bible, s.v. *"huqqâ,"* accessed May 30, 2024, https://www.blueletterbible.org/lexicon/h2708/esv/wlc/0-1/.

5. *Merriam-Webster*, s.v. "ordinance," accessed May 30, 2024, https://www.merriam-webster.com/dictionary/ordinance#synonym-discussion.

6. Wex, s.v. "law," Legal Information Institute, Cornell Law School, updated July 2023, https://www.law.cornell.edu/wex/law.

7. *Merriam-Webster*, s.v. "enable," accessed May 31, 2024, https://www.merriam-webster.com/dictionary/enable.

Chapter 3

1. Blue Letter Bible, s.v. "*stēkō*," accessed May 31, 2024, https://www.blueletterbible.org/lexicon/g4739/kjv/tr/0-1/.

2. *Greek-English Lexicon of the New Testament*, s.v. "ἵστημι," 1889, 308, https://archive.org/details/greekenglishlexi00grimuoft/page/308/mode/2up?view=theater&q=stand.

3. Blue Letter Bible, s.v. "*berit*," accessed June 3, 2024, https://www.blueletterbible.org/lexicon/h1285/kjv/wlc/0-1/.

4. Jeffrey Kranz, "What's a Covenant? A Quick Definition and Overview," OverviewBible, October 20, 2013, https://overviewbible.com/covenant/.

Chapter 4

1. *The New Oxford Dictionary of English*, s.v. "superstition," 2001, https://archive.org/details/newoxforddiction0000unse_g1s3/page/1864/mode/2up?view=theater.

2. Dave Pehling, "Young Girl Who Died During 2021 San Jose 'Exorcism' by Family Members Fought for Her Life, Court Documents Say," CBS News, updated

April 9, 2024, https://www.cbsnews.com/sanfrancisco/news/young-girl-who-died-during-2021-san-jose-exorcism-fought-for-her-life-court-documents-say/.

3. Robert Salonga, "San Jose: Child Exorcism Death Case Headed to Trial," *Mercury News*, May 23, 2024, https://www.mercurynews.com/2024/05/23/san-jose-child-exorcism-death-case-headed-to-trial/.

4. *The New Oxford Dictionary of English*, s.v. "assumption," 2001, https://archive.org/details/newoxforddiction0000unse_g1s3/page/102/mode/2up?view=theater&q=assumption.

CHAPTER 5

1. *The New Oxford Dictionary of English*, s.v. "attitude," 2001, https://archive.org/details/newoxforddiction0000unse_g1s3/page/108/mode/2up?view=theater.

CHAPTER 6

1. "Deployment," U.S. Army, accessed June 4, 2024, https://www.goarmy.com/army-life/intro-to-army-life/deployment.

2. Bible Hub, "1 Corinthians 9:24," accessed June 4, 2024, https://biblehub.com/commentaries/1_corinthians/9-24.htm.

ABOUT THE AUTHOR

ALEXANDER PAGANI IS the founder of Amazing Church in the Bronx, New York. He is an apostolic Bible teacher with keen insight into the realm of the demonic, generational curses, and deliverance. An internationally sought-after conference speaker, he takes an uncompromising approach to the Scriptures and has been involved in more than four hundred deliverance sessions. He has appeared on various television networks, including TBN and The Word Network. An honorary graduate of Central Pentecostal Bible Institute, he carries a spirit of wisdom and discernment to unlock secrets of the kingdom with signs and wonders following his ministry. Pagani is the bestselling author of *The Secrets to Deliverance* and was featured in the 2023 film *Come Out in Jesus Name.* He lives in New York with his wife, Ibelize, and their sons, Apollos and Xavier.

My *FREE GIFT* to You

Dear Reader,

YOUR SOUL HAS BEEN SET FREE IN JESUS'S NAME! I pray that your time reading my book has guided you into a deeper understanding of the steps that come after deliverance as well as a spiritual knowledge that your freedom isn't a one-time experience but rather a daily occurrence.

As a way to show my appreciation for your support, please accept a **FREE** eBook copy of *The Secrets to Deliverance*.

To receive your FREE GIFT, please go to:
MyCharismaShop.com/pages/maintaining-deliverance-freebie.

God Bless Your Soul,

Alexander Pagani

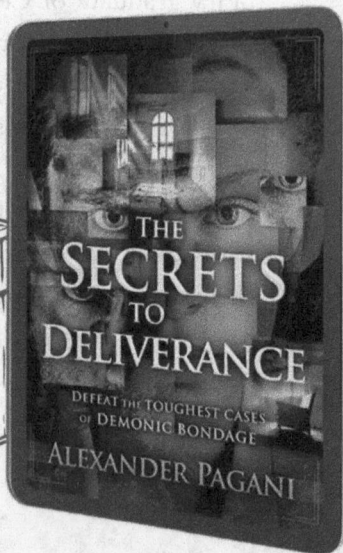

CHARISMA
HOUSE

THE
SECRETS
TO
DELIVERANCE

DEFEAT THE TOUGHEST CASES
OF DEMONIC BONDAGE

ALEXANDER PAGANI

www.ingramcontent.com/pod-product-compliance
Lightning Source LLC
Chambersburg PA
CBHW011159090426
42740CB00020B/3406